BRANT'S
LIGHT

Based on a true story

Dedicated to my children, my light

Love Dad

BRANT'S LIGHT

F.B. Lee

XULON PRESS

Xulon Press
2301 Lucien Way #415
Maitland, FL 32751
407.339.4217
www.xulonpress.com

Printed in the United States of America.

ISBN-13: 978-1-6312-9001-5

TABLE OF CONTENTS

INTRODUCTION

Beware! I feel that before you read this story I should warn you that you can never go back to the way your life was before. You may never see life through rose-colored glasses again. I feel that this story, our story, should have some type of warning as if on a package of cigarettes. That this story could be hazardous to your health. It happened to my children and me. So before you go any further, I need you to know that once you start to read this book you must finish it to the end. I need that kind of commitment from you because I have committed my life and my children's lives to these pages so that you might know that something like this can really happen. I once believed that bad things only happened to bad people. I believed that if you live right, nothing bad will happen to you. Well, this story will tell you the real truth.

For those of you with weak constitutions I suggest you quit reading now. What you will read may very well change your life. That is why I have written it. This story is about good and evil, the light and the darkness. It is a warning to those of you who have never been touched by either or who do not believe in such things. I have seen them both with my own eyes. I have felt the warmth and beauty of pure light, pure goodness. I have also seen pure evil, the darkness of the great beast, the deep dark blackness with fiery red eyes staring back at me. Once you have seen either of these things, your life can never be the same. They leave a mark on your soul that can never be erased.

You will find very little evidence of what I am about to tell you because stories like this do not belong in polite society where everything can be put neatly into a box. Stories like this are usually swept under the rug, left in the dark where society and our government likes them. Even in the town where it happened, you will find very little evidence that my children and I even existed. There are no school records, no police records, not even medical records that any of us existed at all.

What I am about to tell you is between you and me, because I believe that every one of you deserves to hear our story. I will also add, telling this story comes at a very great risk to me, because after all, according to the police and the government, this story never happened. I do, however, want to assure you that this story is true. I still have all the copies of the paperwork in boxes before the courthouse, police department, hospitals, and schools shredded the originals and made us disappear. Today you will find one folder in the courthouse pertaining to our story and it will have one court date on it with no notes. I know this because I have checked.

I am the only one who knows the whole story. There are many who know parts of it but not all. Therefore, it has fallen on me to tell the story. Most of us who have lived through such things never want to talk about it. Many of us would just like to forget it, maybe try to return our lives to normal, whatever that is. But again, we are fooling ourselves, because once you have seen pure good or evil there is no going back. So I will share our story. I am about to tell you things that I do not even like to recall myself; I really do not want to relive what happened. I am telling you our story and reliving it because honestly, once you have lived in fear, it never fades. This story and fear is burned into my memory. The kind of fear where someone holds everything you love in their hand and squeezes it to the point of crushing it, just to control you. This is a fear that I find I cannot run away from nor live with which brings me to our story. So take my hand and let me fearlessly lead you through a story that everyone must know. We all have our demons and the fight against the darkness that happens every day. This story will show you there is hope and you can find the light if only you fight hard enough.

Chapter 1

This story is about my oldest son Brant. I have four children and I have chosen to focus on him. It is not because I love him more or less than my other children, because I love them all the same, with my whole heart, mind, and soul. He was the only one who did not mind being in the story. The rest of the children did not want me to focus on them or to talk much about them at all if I could help it. So I will try to honor their wishes but they will all have their part to play. In order for you to understand my son Brant's life, I feel I should start from the beginning.

My son was born on a chilly October day. He weighed seven pounds twelve ounces and it was one of the happiest days of my life. Little did I know what kind of a man he would become or the influence he would have on me. He had the brightest blue eyes and blonde, nearly white, hair that fanned out in a big afro-like shape, just like a dandelion before the seeds flew. We named him Brant. He had a contagious laugh that somehow struck a funny bone in everyone he met. His smile would light up a room and change the most dreary day into a wonderful adventure. He was a very happy child as well as curious, and he was always getting into things.

I was newly married and my new wife, Martha, had changed somewhat overnight from a very pleasing and happy person to somewhat dark and depressed. Before we were married she always seemed very happy and took great care of me. She always laughed at my jokes and was very agreeable. But that all changed on our wedding night after we left for our honeymoon. In the car on the way to the hotel, out of the blue she looked at me and in a very calm matter-of-fact voice said, "If we ever agree on anything again, I will leave you."

This took me totally by surprise, but she laughed it off like she was joking. I had a sinking feeling that she wasn't. There was something about her tone that frightened me more than it sounded funny. However, I gave a polite laugh and let it go.

I worked long hours on the assembly line making horse trailers and loved to come home to my new baby boy. My wife had informed me, after she had Brant, that she loved babies but as soon as they could walk they would be mine to take care of. I thought she was joking but would soon find out she was very serious about that.

Before we were married Martha and I had talked of dreams of a fairytale life. Neither of us knew what to expect from father and motherhood but we were very excited about it. But as soon as my son came home from the hospital my wife seemed to become depressed and cold. I noticed a darkness in her that I had not seen before. Although she tried to comfort Brant when he cried, she had no patience and if the crying persisted she would quickly hand him off to me. Soon she could not comfort him at all and gave up more easily, to the point that he would not quit crying unless I was holding him. My wife grew to resent Brant for that.

When Brant was about six months old, I noticed that her resentment of him had grown to such a problem that she wanted nothing to do with him at all. She went so far as leaving him in dirty diapers and neglecting him all day until I would get home from work. This made Brant even more happy to see me when I would come home from work. Unfortunately, this reaction made my wife worse. She quit taking care of the house all together and just sat on the couch reading books and watching television while completely ignoring Brant. She had built a small pen with the baby gates for Brant. She left him in there for most of the day and would give him the occasional bottle when he would cry. I had many conversations about how she was treating him but nothing changed.

Until one night I woke up to an awful screaming from Brant's room. I could hear her screaming at him over and over again, "Take your bottle you little bastard!!!" while shoving his bottle into his mouth. I grabbed him from her and asked her what was wrong with her. I told her she could not treat a baby like that. Martha yelled back, "He is no longer my son you take care of the little bastard."

So I did. I would work a ten-hour shift and when I got home I would take care of the housework, supper, and Brant. I could no longer trust her with him in stressful situations so I took care of him when he cried. I also gave him his baths which was great fun for both of us. He loved to take baths. We would spend hours chasing each other around the living room table until Martha would start yelling at us.

Martha had a way of making you feel sorry for her and would cry to get what she wanted. She also loved to blame me for not taking good care of her. I was a new husband and father so what did I know! I thought maybe it was my fault somehow. I was a devout Catholic and did not believe in divorce. She knew this and knowing what I know now she used this against me from the beginning.

After the episodes with Brant, I came to find out that Martha had a nervous breakdown when she was a teenager. It was when her parents got divorced, which also seemed to be a family secret. My mother-in-law accidentally told me about it after I pushed her a bit to find out what was happening with Martha. I wished I knew more about her mental state before I married her but now was too late. So after having brought it up several times, about her getting medical help, I set up an appointment for her with a doctor to see if there was some type of medication to help her with this.

It was time for the appointment. I felt relieved, thinking that morning maybe Martha would finally get what she needed and somehow get things back to normal. Unfortunately, this morning she would not get up to go. So, I picked her up in my arms and carried her out to the car. About halfway there I felt a punch from out of nowhere followed by a wave of hits that caught me totally off guard. I slowly let her to the ground when she jumped up and ran in the house shouting that there was nothing wrong with her and that I was the problem. There was a hatred in her eyes I had not seen before. A narrowing of the eyes that made me feel sick to my stomach. Was she doing this on purpose? Was she really sick or did she like the way things were going? I pushed these thoughts out of my mind. No one could be that evil to hate their own son and like it. Could they? I realized you cannot help someone who does not want help or who is not willing to admit there is something wrong. So I let it go. I was all out of options for now.

However, after that, she got better. She apologized for treating Brant like that and promised that she would be a better mother to him. For a while she did at least start taking care of him while I was gone but there was always a coldness I could see that she had for him no matter how much she tried to cover it up. It was little things at first like trying to feed him baby food he did not like and giving him nothing if he would not eat it. Letting him cry and saying that he should learn how to comfort himself. I could not stand this, I could not listen to him cry without picking him up and comforting him. He would come up to her and hold his arms up for her to hold him and she would turn away from him. It was her way to punish him. I could never understand what she was punishing him for. At the time I thought I was seeing things and dismissed it because who could hate his/her own child.

In my case, I found that being a parent was far more rewarding than I ever thought it could be. From the first moment I saw my son, I realized what love really was. I felt it immediately, a bond that could not be broken, and that red wrinkled up baby was mine. There was nothing I would not do for him. I would put his life before mine and do everything in my power to make his life better.

It came over me like a warm breeze when I held him for the first time. This feeling that no one would harm him if I could help it. I would devote my life to my child even to the point of death. I realized that this is what being a parent is all about; loving your child unconditionally and protecting them with that love from the dark world we live in.

Brant had totally given up on his mother. He no longer asked her for things nor to be held by her. The unsettling thing was Martha was totally fine with this. It seemed that she liked it that way. She did however love to yell at him and punish him for the strangest reasons. She would yell if he did not drink all his bottle or if he drank too much. It was never consistent and I was always confused by her rules. Therefore I knew Brant could not know what he was doing wrong.

Then Martha decided she wanted another baby. I was not at all sure about this because I was starting to get overloaded working all day and taking care of the baby at night. I had seen how she treated Brant and another baby was not the answer. But she was quite persistent and would cry about it and I finally gave in.

Then Brant had a sister, Ann, and again it started all over again, Martha's moodiness and depression. Some days she would not get out of bed. Lucky for me my grandmother lived down the street and would watch the kids on days like this. But my wife had rules about who could come in the house. My family was banned except for my grandmother. She was so patient and kind that no one could say no to her. But the children could only be gone for a certain amount of time and not be returned a minute late, which also complicated matters more.

Brant and my grandmother had great times exploring around the town, which by the way was so small, if you blinked you missed it. That did not stop Brant and Grandma from exploring every inch of the town every day. The town was, to sum it up, a bar and a church. The town was very picturesque; it sat in a small valley by a creek with lots of large cottonwood trees and where you can see the stark white church steeple cross sticking out above the trees. It was a great place to grow up. I was raised Catholic and we always went to church on Sundays. My wife however was usually sick and did not attend. On Martha's bad days, Grandma, Brant, and Ann would go get the mail and go to the park. Brant was a great explorer and Ann was easy because she loved to sleep in her stroller.

After Ann was a couple of months old, I started getting calls at work from Martha that she did not feel that she could handle being around the children. She often told me that she might hurt them. These were horrible phone calls to get in the middle of the day. I worked an hour away and could not just stop off at lunch and check in on them. If it was late in the day I would tell her to put up the baby gates and let the children play and go to her room and read a book until I got home or if it was early enough, I would call Grandma to help. Thank God for Grandma because without her I would not have kept a job with all the work I would have missed.

Then Brant learned how to talk which was great but it also caused problems because he started telling Martha how much fun he had with Grandma. This caused severe tension between my wife and Grandma and the rest of my family. In Martha's mind the children could only have fun with her or me on certain occasions. If they had fun with someone else it infuriated Martha which surprised me because most of the time she did not even like to play with the children. Brant loved to tell about his grand adventures around town with Grandma but while he was telling the stories to his mother, I saw in her face the mounting anger that he was having fun with someone other than her. I knew that someday this would come to an end in a very bad way and there was nothing I could do about it. Brant did not understand that he should not tell his mother about his trips, this was impossible to explain to a four-year-old.

Then one day out of the blue, Martha got into an argument with Grandma. I had never seen anyone yell at Grandma before and it was over literally nothing. I was ashamed that Martha had done it. We had another huge argument over this. It seemed all we did was argue, especially about how she treated the children. Martha loved to fight. I however did not, but this time I was furious and told Martha that if she did not apologize I would leave her. So unwillingly she did.

I decided I needed to ask someone, anyone, for help. I asked my Dad and he reiterated to me what the church says, that is, you should not get divorced. It was very hard to explain to someone what was going on so that they could understand. Because when anyone was around, Martha acted like a totally different person in front of others then how she acted when she was alone with the children and me. How could I expect anyone to understand what was going on when I hardly understood it myself? It was all very unsettling.

I grew up in the Catholic Church and its teachings meant a lot to me. There were very few places where I felt I belonged when growing up but the church was my safe place. I would often pray alone and felt that God could hear me. I had grown up being the "fat" kid in school and when it would get to be too much I would go to church, pray, and feel better. My grandfather broke ground for that very church when he was a young man. My family had knelt and prayed for God's grace for generations. That is what my world was all about; God and family. However to divorce someone, according to the church, would put my soul in jeopardy of going to hell. I also wanted to be a good husband and father. Then there was the question of the children not having a mother or living in a split household. These are questions that I faced daily with no one to guide me and nowhere to find answers to the questions I was asking. To top it off, no one I knew had ever been divorced.

These questions plagued me and every time I made my mind up to leave Martha, she would get better. She would change into a sunshine personality overnight but it would only last days at a time. Just enough to give me hope that everything would be all right. It was as if she knew my every thought and knew just how far to push me, and then reel me back in. I knew my family did not understand it, nor did anyone else, because no one had ever seen this side of her. They only witnessed the nice quiet reserved person. Not the somewhat violent and disturbed person that I saw when everyone went home. It was as if by the closing of the door a dark cloud would appear and choke me and the children.

So I went to Martha's mother for help which would prove to be a very fatal error. But I thought of anyone, she would help me in this situation. Martha would do anything for her mother and her mother should know her better than anyone. Her mother knew of her past, which I did not, because Martha would tell me none of it. Now, I really needed help. Martha had all but alienated me from my family and she had grown so paranoid that she started arguments over nothing. I really had to watch her around the children because she would fly into a rage. Even just because one of the children were staring at her. I could not understand any of what was happening inside her head and what I was seeing with my own eyes. It really did not make sense.

So I had her mother talk to her and Martha and her mother came up with a plan; that was for us to move closer to Martha's family so her mother could help her. Martha came up with all kinds of reasons to move: there were lots of good jobs, her father would let us stay with him, and she would finally get the help she needs. It sounded great to me and frankly, what other options did I have? This situation was pulling my family apart and it was getting so that my own family were scared to stop at my house. Maybe Martha was right, and if it made the kids' lives better, then I was all for it. But there was that nagging voice in my head that said, "Do not go… this is a mistake," but I wanted my marriage to work so I put in my two weeks' notice at work and left.

Chapter 2
MY FATHER-IN-LAW'S

Now, you know that feeling when you get to where you are going and realize it was a huge mistake. That was me when I got to my father-in-law's place. I had only briefly visited him once and had forgotten how small his house was. We would be living in his basement which was two small bedrooms, a bathroom, and a family room. This basement was carved out of rock on the side of a hill in a town that was situated on a hillside. The streets were straight up or down and unknowing to me it was winter nine months out of the year. This was not the paradise they had painted it to be. Not only that but a majority of the jobs were mining gold and they had just decided to close the mine. We were much worse off than before but my wife was overjoyed to be around her mother and family. I thought at least I had that going for me, no yelling for a while.

Unfortunately that lasted only about a week. I moved there with almost no money because my wife was in such a big hurry to get there and with the promise of landing a high-paying job, I initially was not worried. Instead I found myself working on construction crews and finding odd jobs because half the town was out of work. It was into the second week that I realized the reason she did not talk about her dad is because they did not get along. That was something I should have known going into this deal. Martha was in such a big hurry to live by her mother that she decided not to tell me that.

Meanwhile, on the first weekend there I got a phone call in the middle of night after I had just gotten the kids to sleep and after laying concrete block all day. It was my father-in-law calling from the bar totally drunk wanting to know if I could come get him and take him home. I guess now that makes me my alcoholic father-in-law, Dick's, designated driver —as if there are not enough problems already. Soon my wife was just as depressed as ever and had started not getting out of bed unless her mother invited her over.

I also realized that none of her family could stand being around each other for more than a few hours. Any longer than that and there would be war. I soon realized where her violent temper came from. I also found out that her sisters were on medication to keep their anger under control. Unfortunately my wife still believed that there was nothing wrong with her and after a heartfelt talk with her mother, she decided that I was a large part of the problem.

I did not know how much more I could do. I was doing all the cooking, cleaning, and taking care of the children, and working. Martha's mother had turned out to be no help at all and now Martha had an ally that backed up her horrible behavior. My alcoholic father-in-law became a problem as well. He hit Brant's head on the low ceiling after coming home drunk.

At this point, I had had enough! After six long months in that basement, I finally landed a long term job at the electric company and we moved out.

Chapter 3
HOME SWEET HOME

I found a house on the sunny side of the hill which was a lot better than the dark side. It is amazing what sunlight can do to keep your spirits up. The town was beautiful for the three months of summer but the rest of the time it sucked. It had steep side hills with the main road down the middle. This was a real challenge in the wintertime with all the snow and ice. I did not have much money. I could only afford a fixer upper, but the house had potential because it actually had a front yard which was rare. Most of the lots in the area barely had room for the house let alone a yard. The town was old and had been built in the horse and buggy days so the roads were very narrow. However, it was a beautiful town with all the pine trees in the picturesque valley.

Martha was happy at first and things seemed to be going all right but I noticed that her personality split was becoming worse. The out-of-the-house personality was a quiet and reserved housewife. The at-home personality was a mixture of depression and violent bursts of anger. It happened so gradually that we all grew used to it and never realized how bad it had become. The yelling went from once in a while to a dull roar all day long and the reasons for her behavior became so broad and hard to understand, that the children and I became like robots. We did what we were told to

11

avoid conflict and her yelling but it never stopped. Her breakdowns became much more violent and with no reason at all, or reasons that did not make any sense. It seemed to become a way for her to handle stress. Turns out she was always stressed.

When Brant turned five, he loved going on adventures. The town was beautiful in the summer, the air would smell of pine trees and we had a wonderful view of the valley where the town lay. The children loved to go for walks and since town was on a side hill-there were old iron steps up and down the hill between the streets through the pine trees. They loved to run up and down them all the way to the park. Their laughter could be heard up and down the street. These were the best moments, it almost made you forget about the trouble at home. I would often sit on those iron steps in the sunlight with the children and wish it could stay like this. It was so quietand peaceful, except for the children laughing. It made me feel like crying. How had it come to this? We never wanted to go home.

These walks we used to take after work not only gave the children time to be kids but gave Martha alone time which she loved and sometimes made our home life a little better. Soon we had two more children; a boy, Bret and a girl, Lily. Martha loved babies but still wanted nothing to do with them after they turned one year old. In public or in front of her family she acted like the perfect mother even to the point of smothering the children with affection. This was very confusing for the children because a bulk of our time was spent at home where she rarely ever even spoke to them other than yelling.

Now with 4 kids, our home life was getting increasingly worse. It was hard for me to control her around the children. Her violent bursts of anger were getting worse. Martha had started throwing temper tantrums like a small child. She would stomp her feet and start throwing things at the children. At first she would miss them but I noticed she was aiming closer and closer to the child before I could stop her. Until finally one day she hit Bret in the face on the chin which got him five stitches. Martha cried and cried and said it was an accident, but was it? I was finding it harder and harder to believe her bouts of crying and excuses.

Birthday parties were the worst. Martha loved to have her family over for the kids' birthday parties. None of the children were allowed to bring other kids over because Martha could not handle it. The house would have to be cleaned top to bottom. It was a nightmare for the two weeks leading up to a birthday party. The yelling would hit a high note and we were constantly on edge for the next rage-induced attack. She would sit on her throne in the living room and bark orders. It was futile to try to make her happy. Not only was it impossible to get all these tasks she set upon us done but it had to be her way which was different every time.

Then the party day would finally arrive and with it her family. Martha would always be in a wonderful mood and cooking lots of food like she was a Suzy Homemaker. However the children and I would sit back and get a chance to relax a little because we knew she would not lose it with her family there. That night would be our first night of sleep in weeks and finally the house would be quiet. The children and I hated birthday parties. Martha seemed to suck the life out of everything she touched.

Martha loved to be in control and if anything threatened that, she would lose it. Brant was a wonderful son and he was always making little cards or coloring pictures and writing I love you on them even when it was not a holiday. I used to love getting cards from him and telling him how good of a job he had done on it. But he was always trying to please his mother and making her cards. I began to hate this. Not hating that he made her a card, because that was a wonderful thing for a child to do, but it was what Martha would do to him every time she received something from him.

Brant would come running up to her with one of his masterpieces which he would spend days making and Martha would always cut him down. She would either point out that he colored out of the lines or spelled a word wrong. I never heard her say nice words like how much she liked it or even acknowledge he did a good job. She would just demoralize him over and over again. I watched his little smile turn into a frown and usually tears as he ran to his room downstairs. I would follow him and put my hand on his shoulder and tell him it was all right and that he had done a good job. But I could see the pain in his eyes and I knew there was nothing I could do to make that pain go away. I knew someday I would have to end this suffering. Sometimes I would notice a cruel smile on Martha's face as Brant ran away crying, but surely I was just seeing things. After all, what mother would make a child cry on purpose.

When Brant was turning five, he developed a stuttering problem. If I had I known at the time that this was a sign of abuse, I might have understood better how to prevent it. That would be by keeping him away from his mother, which I did anyway. I never knew anyone who had this problem before and therefore thought it was just a phase he was going through. Martha had no patience for his stuttering and would yell at him to quit it until he could not talk at all.

She eventually quit talking to him altogether and told him to only talk to his father and that she did not want to talk to a "dummy." I felt so bad for Brant and worked with him to get him over it. When he started school, they informed us that Brant may have to be in a special class because of his stuttering. However, once in school, his stutter suddenly disappeared. Little did I know it was more likely the fact that his mother no longer talked to him and he was mostly away from her at school which made the stuttering go away.

Chapter 4

GRADE SCHOOL

B rant loved school. Not only did he see and socialize with other kids but when in school, he did not have to be around his mother. This was a horrible thing to say but it was still very true. Brant made many friends. He was always joking around and trying to make everyone smile. I do not know where he found the drive to be happy the way things were at home. He would always go out of his way for other kids and if they had trouble with some kind of schoolwork he would help them out. He would hold doors for people and compliment everyone. He carried his heart on his sleeve which made him an easy target for bullies. But he did not let them get him down.

The teachers loved him and gushed about him every time we went to parent teacher conferences. He seemed to make everyone happy. Martha would always try to take credit that he took after her. This made me sick. If anything, she did her best to destroy him every chance she got. Immediately after these conferences, after taking credit for the wonderful son he was, she would tear him down, telling him his grades, which were A's, were not good enough and that the teachers did not like him. It was better just to let her get it over with. She could not handle Brant doing well. It always made her fly into a tantrum. Brant and I had a system we would let the yelling go on. Then after she had gone to bed I would tell him what the teachers really had said and tell him how good a job he was doing. It only made it worse to engage in an argument in an attempt to make her stop. I had found that yelling, which would last for days on end, would be over in an hour or so if I did not interrupt. She had worn me down to only fighting the fights that I felt important enough to battle. And I had to pick my battles carefully.

I noticed as the children got older that the more time they spent away from Martha the happier they were. Brant became very interested in becoming healthy he was always doing push -ups and running at home. He soon discovered baseball and loved being on a team. He had a lot of friends but always picked the wrong kid for a best friend because every time he found one they moved away. It did not help that Martha had banned him from staying overnight at friends' houses and did not allow him to go to birthday parties. He was also never allowed to have friends over because Martha would never let anyone but family in our house. By now it was going around that the children's friends were scared of Martha. One of the children had brought a friend by after school because they thought Martha would not be home. They soon realized she was when the yelling started. It frightened the poor child so much that the rumors started that Martha was scary.

The children were never allowed to have friends over mostly because our house was always a mess. I cleaned it on the weekends when I was not working but that was the only time it was clean. One time I left it. I thought if it gets dirty enough Martha would clean it because she was a germaphobe. I was wrong, she cleaned her spot around her chair and between her and the TV because she had to watch her shows. After every dish was dirty I thought finally she would clean but instead I came home from work and found out she had bought paper plates. I could not stand it anymore and stayed up half the night cleaning up. I felt bad for my children to have to live like this so I did the best I could.

That was the way it was. She would sit on her throne and bark orders all day long. She would make the children take care of themselves and bring her drinks and snacks to her chair while she watched television. She was the only one who got snacks of any kind because they were hers and no one could have them. This was very hard for a child to understand and punishment was harsh.

If one thing was not done exactly as she wanted it, like folding a towel wrong or putting a dish in the wrong place, it would have to be done all over again until it was done right. That is after the loud yelling and screaming was over. I would step in to try to stop the lunacy but found after a while it did no good. I was not a fighter and she loved it and I soon found there was no way to beat her in an argument. Because even if I won an argument she would take it out on the children when I was not around which made it even worse. So I would step between her and the child and take over the job that he/she should have been doing and finish it for them.

This really infuriated Martha. She told me often that I loved the children more than I loved her. I would say nothing. At least this changed the focus of anger towards me and not the children. I could see it in their faces, it was the look of prisoners, dull and passive, in a nightmare that never ended. It had happened so slowly over so many years that I had not noticed how bad it had become. We were prisoners, the children hated it here and so did I but what was I supposed to do. Her violent rage towards the children, especially Brant, was out of control.

There were always accidents that happened while I was at work; like someone fell down the steps and got bruised up or hit their head somehow. I never thought about it. Martha always had a good explanation for it and children did get hurt while they were playing. Once Bret got his head slammed in the sliding door on the van and got a concussion. Brant and Ann were always bruised up from supposedly falling down the stairs. I questioned Martha every time but there was always a reason and she always took them

Chapter 5

JUNIOR HIGH

B rant was getting into junior high school now and things at home were worse than they had ever been. I knew that this would happen when the children became teenagers because Martha was losing control of them. The children were finding out from their friends that their mother was not normal. The way she treated them was not right. Martha's attacks on the children had gotten more frequent and much more violent. There were times I had to bodily stop her from hurting them.

Then it happened one evening, Ann was lying on the floor and for no reason what so ever Martha jumped out of her chair ran over and kicked Ann like you would a football and she flew against the wall. I was between them before she tried to kick Ann again. It was all I could do to stop her from doing it again. I yelled, "What are you doing!"

Martha replied, "Did you see the way that bitch looked at me! You always stick up for your precious children you rotten bastard!" then she stormed out of the room. The look in Martha's eyes stopped me cold. They were bloodshot and narrowed and she was biting her lower lip, kicking with all she had. She wanted to inflict as much pain as possible with those kicks on her own daughter. I knew then in these fits of rage she would kill.

I asked Ann if she was all right after she quieted down and she said she was. Ann was thirteen at the time and a day later she got sick on the way home from volleyball. I wanted to take her to the doctor but Martha said she would. She started becoming violent again. So I let her take Ann to the doctor so it would not provoke her to attack one of the children again, because at this point anything was possible. I called my mother-in-law and told her she needed to go with Martha and Ann to the doctor after I told her what had happened.

I needed help and my mother-in-law, Pam, always said that if Martha was out of control to call her and she would help. I got home from work the next day and they were both waiting for me. They told me nothing was wrong with Ann and that she was just fine. My mother-in-law pulled me aside before she left and told me I should not be telling her lies about her daughter and what a horrible husband I had been for saying such things. Now I knew that there would be no help. I would have to do it on my own. My children's lives were at stake. I had been seeing a lawyer in town for an automobile accident I had been in so I decided to see what my chances of getting full custody in a divorce would be. I had had enough.

Chapter 6

WRONG MOVE

I hired a lawyer in town to handle a fender bender that I had been in with a young girl who did not have a driver license. I received some injuries in the accident and as anyone knows these type of cases take a long time. The lawyer I hired was known as 'the judge' because he also served as a judge in the town and had since retired and was practicing law on the side. I knew him for quite a few years before I hired him and considered him more of a friend than an acquaintance. He was very well liked in the community and I was told he was a man of high morals.

He was a large stately man with the kind of office a judge would have with the big desk and lots of book cases. We had been talking about the case and were about to wrap it up. I had been trying to work it into the conversation but ran out of time so I asked him hypothetically if a man could get full custody of his kids. He dropped the pencil he had been writing with and bluntly said no. It was so abrupt it startled me. He then told me before I could say anymore that he had to go. He had an appointment somewhere else and needed to leave immediately. I thought this was all very strange but that maybe I was reading more into it than I should have.

I finished out the rest of the day at work. I trudged up the stairs and noticed it was very quiet in the house, no yelling just silence. At this point, I knew something was not right. I had just reached the top of the stairs when I saw Martha. She had a rather disturbing look on her face. It looked like a rattle snake right before the bite. Her eyes were narrowed again and her lips were pursed so tight they were white. Satan himself would be scared. She asked me where I had been and I told her that I had been to the lawyer and had gone back to work to finish up the day. Immediately she was in my face, nose to nose, she said in her harsh cutting voice, "So you think you can leave me do you?"

She knew! How was this possible? I had just talked to the lawyer no more than a couple hours ago and somehow she knew everything. I could see it again in her face. She wanted to inflict pain, to kill even! It was the same look I had seen on her face when she attacked Ann. I looked around, I saw no knife or gun. Then she smiled a smile that made me feel sick and then Martha said, "You will never beat me in court and what do you think will happen to your precious children if you are not around to protect them." She smiled wickedly again and walked out of the room.

I did not know what to say or do I just stood there like someone just hit me with a bat. Not only did my lawyer break the law and his code of ethics by telling people what I told in confidence, but I just learned that if she could get to the judge like that, then who could I go to for help? I felt a lot like Jimmy Stewart in "It's a Wonderful Life" when he found out he had never been born. The next day I looked around the town I had lived in for fourteen years and realized I had never really seen it before. It was a giant cage like a prison, just like a gold fish in a bowl and the children and I were trapped. How could we escape if the judge would do something like that? If the judge was on her family's side, then surely the police would be too.

I was dumbfounded. I knew I had very little chance of getting full custody before now. Now I realized my chances were almost zero. I also realized that nothing had been an accident. She had all but admitted that she hurt the children on purpose and these so called accidents had all been lies. She truly was a monster. She was not human. She was like some demonic evil beast from hell and if she did those things when I was around, then what was she doing when I was at work? My head hurt and my stomach was in knots and that is when I realized I was done. I would start planning our escape. But the next time, I would be all in, live or die. I would save the children from her. For now she had won but I knew the day was coming when there would be no choice and I must be ready for it. Divorce did not matter to me anymore. I would rather go to hell for protecting my children than to do nothing. After all, that is what being a parent is, giving my life, mortal or eternal, for my child's well-being.

So I began searching the internet trying to find anything to help me. There was absolutely nothing. Not only that but I found out in my state the mother was always favored at least two-to-one against the father's parental rights. If a mother wanted custody here, she always got it no matter what. I was stunned to say the least. There were no websites for a dad trying to save his children from an abusive mother but there were literally hundreds for women and children with abusive husbands. My odds now seemed to be in the negative of even getting partial custody but I would be ready anyway. I would not give up until the children were safe somehow.

Meanwhile, Brant joined the cross country team and continued playing baseball and despite what was happening at home, he became very popular. He had excellent grades too and the teachers all loved him. He was constantly cheering his teammates on no matter if they played the whole game or not at all. That was what made him special and everyone loved him for it. I never heard him say an unkind word about anyone. That's just the way he was. He was an excellent runner and medaled in almost every event. Soon he had his own little fan club of little kids following him around. He would love answering their questions about how to run faster.

It was amazing to watch this boy who had so many problems at home show nothing but love and compassion for everyone he met. He had a way of casting this beautiful white light everywhere he went. I would watch him walk into a crowd of quiet kids and within minutes they would all be laughing their heads off. It was a gift he had and a way about him that inspired people. He made everyone feel special. He gave us what we all needed, someone to believe in us or just a kind gesture.

Brant was also a very religious person. Religion was a large part of our life. I remember waiting in the church parking lot for about an hour one day while Brant held the door for everyone to leave. He always looked out for everyone else. It was the way he was wired to help people. His brain did not work like most people. School was easy for him and seemed to be another of his super powers. He used it to tutor students on his own time. He was always helping some friend with a difficult assignment. Everyone was his friend so this kept him busy all the time. Teachers would often say how he would think outside of the box and come up with ideas that frankly some of the teachers did not understand. But they were amazed by it. He also had no fear of speaking in front of people and won several awards for speeches he gave. He had found an outlet for all his gifts that his mother could never see. Instead of becoming dark like her he became a light for all to see no matter what she did to him. I was very proud of him, more so than anyone else, because I alone knew what he faced every day and he still managed to shine his light in spite of it. I loved him dearly for this.

Chapter 7

HIGH SCHOOL BASEBALL

B rant entered high school. He was a skinny kid, about five foot five and weighed about a hundred pounds but he was all heart. No matter what he did he gave one hundred and ten percent. He loved the baseball team and they loved him back. The team he played on were all older kids except for him he was the only freshman on the team. The older boys had accepted him into the pack and Brant loved it.

When Brant became a freshman most of the team were seniors and they had a lot of talent but seemed to never have a winning season. They had gotten a new coach the year before Brant arrived and that helped some but they seemed to be missing something. The only thing different this year was Brant. Just looking at Brant you would think that they should definitely hide that little kid so he will not get hurt. He looked like a small mouse in the cat's den out on the field but it seemed the team changed having Brant there. I know how it sounds, but you had to be there to see it.

The team won a few games the past season, which was a lot more than usual, but there seemed to be an element that was not there before. When Brant shouted, hitters began hitting and the good hitters started getting home runs. Now to watch the game was really quite amazing. Many times a batter would be down two strikes and you could hear Brant shout, "You can do it!" and sure enough every time they did. Kids that had never hit before were knocking the ball into the outfield. It was extremely fun to watch. Brant would get his fair share of play time, maybe a little less because he was the youngest one on the team, but it was not his playing that was helping win the game. It was that special light that was helping them win. Something you just could not quite put your finger on. That special something that was like a feeling of excitement in the air.

I always kept what I was thinking to myself because maybe it was just a father being biased and seeing more than what was happening. Then one day the new coach came up to me and told me that maybe Brant should be coaching the team because whatever he was doing was a big part of why they were winning. He went so far as to tell me he was the heart of the team. He said this team was playing way beyond any expectations anyone had for them. They went from being a mediocre team to having a winning season. Brant's winning personality seemed to energize the entire team. Many of them came up to me and told me that if Brant had not shouted at them and encouraged them the way he had, they would never have made the play.

No matter how far behind or ahead the team got, you would find Brant hanging on the fence shouting his lungs out at the players. Always words of encouragement and if someone struck out he would always pat them on the back and tell them better luck next time. They were all very afraid of disappointing Brant because he was their number one fan. The team was getting better and better because of the kid on the fence.

Then one day, out of the blue, Brant told me that they would be the region champions. I did not want him to get his hopes too high and told him winning a few games is great but winning the championship is something else. I said, "You are expecting a lot from these guys. I mean, they had already won more games this year than they have the last three years put together, but they have never come this close to a region championship."

He just gave me his award winning smile and a wink and said, "All I have to do is tell them they can do it and they will."

I said, "Ok good luck with that just don't be let down if it does not happen. You guys have played way beyond what anyone expected and your all winners in my book."

Well, guess what? They would go on to win the region championship against teams they had played in previous years and have never come close to beating. They were not even rated at the beginning of the season. You might think that that little kid had nothing to do with it, but he was the only thing different on that team. I saw plays that you did not even see in the big leagues by a bunch of kids that had talent but had never showed it.

They had needed a leader, someone to believe in them. I cannot tell you how many times I saw the batter look at Brant and dig in for a hit. It was as if the batter needed Brant to give him the ok to hit it out of the park. He made them become more and do more than they ever thought possible. Maybe that was why the teamed named Brant the most valuable player. You may say it was just a fluke, but as it turns out, that is not the only team Brant would be on that would win a championship that nobody thought they could win either.

Later on that summer I got a boat from my brother that he was not using. After working on the motor for a month or so I decided to take the kids to the lake for some boating. Martha was sick and did not want to go but the children were very excited about it. It was about an hour drive to the lake and the kids were having more fun than I had ever remembered but that was the way that it was when Martha was not around.

It was a beautiful day and thankfully the boat did not sink and the motor did not quit so it was great. We spent the entire day boating all over the lake and the kids were loving it. We did not really want it to end. On the way home we stopped for ice cream but as we climbed back in to head home the fun ended. The vehicle grew quiet because we knew what we were heading back to. Later on the counselors would ask if they had any happy memories from their childhood with Martha. They would answer the only fun time they could remember was the day she stayed home and we went to the lake. When we got home the kids could not contain themselves and told Martha how much fun they had. Martha flew into a rage that the children had that much fun without her and we were never allowed to go boating again.

Chapter 8
CROSS COUNTRY

I knew Brant started running cross country to get away from his mother. I knew because I had hinted to him that if he was not home Martha could not hurt him. It was a horrible thing to do but what choice did I have. Brant knew, as did I, that every moment at home with her was dangerous to his health. I am pretty sure he did not know he would be good at running. It turned out he was really good at it. Just watching this sport made me tired, I never knew anyone who did this sport before. When I got to his first meet, I decided Brant really hated his mother to run this particular race. It looked endless, little lines on the grass around the golf course with cones marking the turns and some school official driving a golf cart making the leaders chase him up and down the field of green.

Now I have heard a lot of people say how out of shape high school kids are. I am pretty sure they have never been to a cross country meet! Most of those people saying that, would not make it halfway through the race, which is a little over three miles. That is a long way in any book. These kids run it for a little medal the size of a quarter. As far as I am concerned, any kid who runs cross country should get a medal whether they win or lose because each race is an accomplishment.

That being said Brant was fast, not number one every time but always in the top twenty which is awesome when you are running against anywhere from forty to one hundred of the fastest kids in the state at any one time. It was not just that he placed in nearly every race he ever ran, but it was the way he ran.

The first time I saw the course I thought great, another sport that was like watching paint dry! Then they lined the kids up. They are in all different colors against the green backdrop of usually a golf course and then the gun goes off. It was an awesome sight to get up on a small hill and look down at all those different sized kids in brightly colored uniforms take off in a big bunch across the green. It was the perfect backdrop with the perfectly cut green grass and the miles of shelter belts and ponds to help mark the path. By the end they could be strung out for a mile looking for the finish line. But that was not what got me. What got me was the way he ran.

I still get a lump in my throat when I think about it. He had the perfect running form. He did not make it look easy but his running was smooth and flawless like a deer running through the meadow. It was if he was born to run. Not that he necessarily liked running but he was good at it. He actually told me that himself. I could also see something that no one else knew. The look on his face was not just that of a runner giving it all he had. I saw the boy running from his mother helping relieve the strain she put on him every day and knowing in this moment he was in control and he was able to push her out of his mind. On this field, in these moments, he could be Brant, he can be carefree, because Martha was nowhere in sight.

However, to the outside world he looked like a boy giving it his all. Only he and I knew he needed to run to keep his sanity, for in our world, there really was none. We just tried to do the best we could. I loved these meets; to get the opportunity to spend time with my son away from his mother. Because she never wanted to go to his meets and frankly, that was just fine with us. When we would drive home, we would always stop somewhere to eat. I would usually hide- away a few dollars now and again, since Martha controlled all the money, so we could get a treat like ice cream or something on the way home. Our relationship seemed less strained on these trips but I could always tell there was something always bothering him. Something he wanted to tell me but no matter how I tried to get him to open up, he never did.

He became popular at his school because they had never really had a good cross country runner. The little kids would always be coming up to him and telling him how great he had done and there was never a time that I did not see him stop and talk to them. No matter if he was running late and needed to go, Brant was always doing things like that. Many times I would wait for him because he was talking to some little kids about the race. It always made me smile, here was my son with more things wrong in his life than anyone knew, and yet he still took the time to stop. No matter what, at any cost. Because, of course, Martha always timed us and knew exactly when we should be home and a minute late could cost Brant dearly.

I would always make up an excuse why we were late but there would always be retaliation. There was always a price to pay with her if you broke her rules. I found this out the hard way many times. And if she could not retaliate against me, she would retaliate against the children. She would always use them against me as a means to control me and to keep me in line. I knew there was nothing she was not capable of. I saw it in her face more often now. That darkness, the narrow eyes the pursed lips, just waiting to attack. No one ever believed me when I told them just how far she was willing to go. But then again why would they? No one ever saw the real Martha, just me and the children.

Brant also started an acting career. He was in his first play and played the role of Raggedy Andy. I had no idea he could act and he did a wonderful job. It was crazy to think that a boy who spent his whole life hiding his emotions could express himself so well as someone else. Brant would go on and act in every play throughout his high school years and would only get better the older he got. He really had talent. It seemed no matter what he tried he was at least good at it. His potential seemed limited only to what his mind could dream up. It was exciting as a parent just to see what he would come up with next. I had always known he was meant for something special. I felt that he could do anything and that his future would be full of promise if I could keep him away from his mother.

Chapter 9

THE INCIDENT

Things had been getting worse, the older the children got the more vicious Martha became. She was losing her control over them and it was driving her mad. They were getting bigger and starting to fight back enough to protect themselves from her and she did not like that. Somewhere along the way punishment had accelerated to the point where she was not finished until the child cried. She said horrible things to them. Such things that you would not tell your worst enemy. Her attacks had become daily and I was at the point of sitting on the edge of my seat so I could stop her from hurting them. I soon realized she was at the breaking point. I told the children to stay in their rooms and convinced Martha that this was good for them, to keep them out of her way. This was the only way I could protect them.

It got so bad that I had finally started living with the children in the basement. Our house had a main floor and a walk out basement. Martha never liked going down there and the boys had their room down there. I starting taking the children down there and eating with them and watching movies. So we essentially lived down there. I found it much easier to protect them from her and we could be more ourselves without her seeing us. Because we had become separate identities now too. There was us outside the house and us inside the house. We could laugh and play and talk outside but inside the house you stayed quiet so as not to awaken the dragon upstairs. There was always tension in the house. The kind that you could feel like a weight around your neck. When the door closed, darkness came with it. In the basement we could laugh with each other and try to have a little fun watching movies. However if we laughed too loud or made too much noise the yelling and screaming would start, so we knew our limits.

This seemed to work for a few years as I had talked Martha into letting us stay down there. I had told her it made sense because the children could not annoy her this way. It worked well until one day she got jealous of me spending time with the children and it was over just like that. She told me I needed to spend more time with her which meant staying upstairs and watching television with her. It was too bad because then the children would come up to play with me and this would set Martha off every time. So much for our quiet time alone. It was like playing chess but all the other side had was an army of queens.

Most of my family were scared to come and visit because Martha was getting bolder with them and made it uncomfortable, to say the least, when they would come. I would have relatives stop by and would be forced to not let them in the house because I was scared at what my wife would say to them. She was always in a bad mood and our house became off limits to everyone.

At this time I could no longer even slow Martha down. She often referred to our daughters as, "whores and bitches" and the boys were always "bastards." I would stop her time and again trying to hurt them and the kids were scared to be around her. I just could not understand why she was doing this. How could a parent be so cruel to her own children? It just did not make sense. I had never known anyone who hated their own children. My parents may have been strict and spanked us, but I know it was only to teach us right from wrong not because they liked it. I had nothing to compare this too. I grew up on a farm and the only thing that would kill its young was a mad sow, a female pig. These unfit mothers went to market as soon as sale day came. Marriage is supposed to be about love and commitment. Any children you have you should love more than yourself. This was not our case. It was upside down and inside out.

Martha had lied from the beginning. She had found out just how and what could keep me trapped to her. The children were only a means to control me. She hated them. I had seen this on many occasions. She kept them around so that people would think she was normal and to make her mother happy. She had kept me with her with lies and tears and when that no longer worked she used the children against me. She knew I could never get full custody and therefore she would always have access to them. Beating them was stress relief for her and a way to keep me in line. She knew I would never leave them with her alone because it would tear me apart.

Our house had become some deep dark ominous cavern and we were slaves to serve the dragon, the great beast with her red eyes shining in the darkness. She controlled us in her walls and tormented our dreams. Many nights I would wake up in a cold sweat from nightmares of what she would do to the children once I was gone.

Yet in public she controlled herself. Many times I would lose my patience with her and yell at her to not call the children such horrible names and to not attack them. She would only smile, that wicked smile, like she knew something I did not know. It made me sick. I knew she would make the children pay for me speaking out. I had thought of taking the children and running but where could we go where they would not find us? What if I got caught? Then the children would have no one and Martha could do what she pleased with them. I could not bear to live with that in a cell thinking about it all day. So I went on waiting for the day it would blow up and I knew it would come. This is when I grew physically sick. Living like this was getting to me physically. I was diagnosed with heart problems and stomach ulcers. She was slowly killing me by using my love for my children against me.

Then Ann got a letter in the mail from the state teen committee. They wanted her to be a pageant contestant and to come to the state capital to compete. Ann was very excited about this so we decided to make the trip. I had hoped that some time away would slow Martha down. Brant, Bret, and Lily would stay with their grandparents while we were away.

We arrived and received Ann's itinerary and went ahead and got a room. Ann was very excited. The girls spent the day getting ready for a show they would put on later that afternoon. There was nothing to see until later that night and it was a beautiful day so Ann said I could go ahead and do some fishing, so I did, while Martha laid down for a nap. After all, nothing was going on and Martha and Ann would not be anywhere near each other, so what could go wrong?

I left and sat on the river bank and caught more fish than I had ever caught before. I could not keep up taking the fish off and baiting my hook. It had been a wonderful day. The weather had been perfect and the fish were biting for a change and I was in a good mood.

Martha should have gotten her alone time and maybe for once everything would be ok. But as I got into the hotel I could hear it. Someone was yelling and it was that familiar yell that had grown to be daily noise for sixteen years.

I could hear the yelling through the door and so could a lot of the other guests because it had attracted quite a crowd. I pushed my way to the door and went in and found Martha screaming at Ann. "You little bitch you always get your way!" and with that Ann ran into the bathroom and locked the door tears on her face.

I looked directly at Martha and said, "What did you do?"

Martha yelled back, "That bitch would not let me fix her hair the way I wanted it! She wanted it a different way!"

I could not believe it, this was over hair. I said, "You do realize everyone in the hotel heard you. This is one of the most important days in your daughter's life and you have single-handedly destroyed it. You should be ashamed of yourself." She had gone too far and I was mad.

Martha charged at me, pushing me into the wall while yelling in my face, "Don't you ever talk to me like that again or I will make sure that rotten bitch pays for it! You cannot be there to protect her all the time!"

At this point, Ann ran out of the bathroom and out the door while I had Martha occupied. I thought to myself smart girl get out while the coast was clear. It was time for the show to start. So after Martha cooled off we went out. I am sure she would not have gone but her family showed up so she went with them. It was a wonderful show full of singing and dancing by the contestants. You would have never known what had happened earlier by looking at Ann. She was having a great time. Unfortunately we had gotten used it and we must always keep up appearances no matter what. My parents had come and gone and Ann and I left Martha with her family and went to the room to go to bed. We would leave early the next day.

The next day Martha started yelling immediately, still mad from the day before, saying all the horrible things she could think of to Ann. I got about three miles out of town when Martha realized she had forgotten her program and wanted to go back for it. Martha started to blame Ann for this and I had had enough. I stepped on the brakes and stopped in the middle of the road.

I looked over at Martha and said, "I have had enough yelling! I cannot stand it anymore! You will not say another word or I will leave you right here on the side of the road!" Martha opened her mouth to yell and I cut her off. I said, "Not one word! You have ruined your daughter's special day and so help me I will drag you kicking and screaming out of this car and leave you in the ditch."

The look on my face must have read volumes because she turned away and said not a word the rest of the trip.

From then, it was the most peaceful trip I had had in years. I looked in the rear view mirror and could see a small hidden smile on Ann's face and that look also had made me feel better than I had in years. I managed to make Martha quiet for once. I knew the retaliation would be horrific but for this moment we won. I wish Brant was here he would have probably laughed out loud. Lord knows I wanted to. When we got home it was business as usual and the yelling started and never stopped. Martha however did not try to attack the children for a while evidently this incident had slowed her down.

Chapter 10

BRANT AND ANN'S ULTIMATUM

A few days later Martha was watching her favorite murder mystery show on television, which was usually all she ever watched. I was pretty sure that if I was ever found dead they would never find out what killed me because she had watched about a thousand shows like this which in a way shows you how to kill someone and get away with it. At this time, I was sure I was at the top of list of people to knock off. I was sure one day they would find me and the children stabbed to death in our sleep, sad but true, but this was nothing new to me.

I was probably the only adult who knew Martha was capable of killing. I had seen it in her eyes when she attacked the children. That cold heartless narrowing of the eyes and I had seen in earlier attacks. There was no remorse in them. They were cold and heartless and just evil, pure evil. It is hard to describe unless you have seen it yourself. The kind of look that makes the hair on your neck stand up and you know you are or will be fighting for your life. She never ever apologized for her actions like she did when we were first married. I had felt her kicks and punches several times when I stopped her attacks against the children. They had left large bruises on my body let alone on the children's. Her intention was to inflict as much damage as she possibly could because she never knew if

I would stop her from connecting with one of her blows. Martha weighed around two hundred pounds and she had quite a punch. If Ann had been kicked a little higher she might not be here today or if that toy would have hit Bret a little harder it would have been more than stitches.

However to me the part that was really disturbing was that she was only dangerous to me and the children. She had held several jobs with small children and was currently helping teach preschool. It was very hard to watch her have so much patience with someone else's children and none with her own. I could not even imagine what the children thought of her after they saw her being so nice to total strangers. It was horrible.

Anyway, while Martha was so engrossed with watching her murder show and how the murderer had actually done it, Ann motioned to me and told me she had to show me something downstairs. She grabbed me by the hand and led me downstairs to the only room in the house where you could not hear what was being said upstairs. Only the children and I knew this because we had tested it so that we could have conversations without Martha hearing it. The children saved these conversations for very important reasons because if Martha found out it would not be good for any of us.

Brant was waiting in the room when we arrived and closed the door behind us. I knew this was very important because these two rarely agreed on anything and I had never seen them work so well together. Brant and Ann told me they had enough. They had devised a plan of emancipation from their parents and had a paper they had for me to sign so they could leave the house. They found a place to stay and had it all planned out. They had a couple of friends who had done the same thing with their parents and they had their own place. They told Brant and Ann that they could stay with them. I was stunned, this was it the day I knew would come. What Brant and Ann did not realize is that those kids parents did not want anything to do with them. They had actually moved out of town and left their kids there with their grandparents. Martha would never let them go. She needed to control them.

I had been waiting for this moment for sixteen years and now it was here. A million things went through my mind. They did not know what they were asking. I found out the hard way years before how hard it would be to leave her based on the first time I tried. She would never let them go, not like this and if she found out, who knows what she would do to them. So I decided right then and there, I had gone over this in my head for years, decided if I do this, there would be only one outcome. I would have to win full custody or die trying. There would be no middle ground. I had realized a long time ago that I could never drop them off and leave them with their mother alone and wait to see what she would do to them. I was sure that this would be the ultimate retaliation and I was sure she would murder them.

I paused while I thought all this out and then I asked them, "If I divorce her will you stay with me." They looked at each other with a sigh of relief. They obviously did not know for sure if their plan would work. But to me the mere fact that they were willing to throw their lives to the wind just for a chance to escape her told me all I needed to know. I knew that they would have to be as devoted as I was on getting them away and safe from her. We would have to stick together or this would never work because I knew we were on our own.

Had I known everything that would happen, I might have just ran with them and took my chances. I realized we were up against a stacked deck. There would be no help from the local police so I would have to go higher in the government to even have a prayer. I knew this because my father-in-law's drinking buddies were on the police force and everyone in town knew them. Their family had been there for years. Martha's family was on the hospital board, the school board, and most of them worked for the city. I knew there would be no help because the most influential man in town, the judge, had told Martha's family about me just asking about custody in a divorce.

Suddenly Brant and Ann's faces relaxed, then they both said, "We are so glad you're on our side. Mom always said that you knew everything she did and approved of all the beatings she gave us and that if we ever told you it would get a lot worse."

I asked them what they were talking about. They commenced to tell me of hundreds of beatings from Martha. She would push them down the stairs, following them down punching and kicking them until one of the other children dragged them away. She would also hit them, not in the face so anyone would see, but in the stomach and the back until Martha got tired of hitting them.

Then they told me that she would not let them have any food unless I was home from work. The rest of the time she starved them. Everything was beginning to make sense. I had found food wrappers in the kids closet and I had also seen the look in their eyes like they hated me. I felt the anger mounting, it was all I could do not to go up there and punch her like she had punched them. She had used us against each other for all these years. No wonder I could see the resentment in their eyes and that they always seemed to want to tell me something.

Martha was a monster. She was like the fictional monster under the bed that all children read about and fear, but this one was real. I hated her more in that moment than I could have ever hated anyone. I yelled, "You mean she did all this?" Ann put her hand over my mouth and whispered "Shh, you are way too loud." My blood was boiling, while I was working so she could stay at home with the kids she had been beating and starving them this whole time. What was worse she had told them that I knew about it! This whole time I thought I had been protecting them, she had been beating and starving them every chance she could when I was not around. It was all a lie everything she had ever said was a lie.

I looked at Brant and Ann and told them I was so sorry for everything that had happened and that I would get them away from her. I promised them I would keep her from hurting them. I had never seen them more relieved in my life. They actually had color in their faces that I was on their side. I needed to do something but knew the consequences. I realized that this promise would put us all to the test. I put my hand on each of their shoulders and told them to stay away from her and to not take the chance of letting her know anything was up. This was going to have to be our secret because if Martha found out, their chance at freedom would be over. Our only hope was surprise. Without it, I would disappear in jail or worse and she would have the children all to herself. God help us because he was the only one who could.

Chapter 11

ESCAPE

After the earlier incident with the judge I had convinced Martha that I needed a new lawyer because it was taking too long. So I got a new lawyer as far away as possible in a larger town fifty miles away which was quite a pain because of the distance. But I knew when the time would come to file for a divorce, I would need a lawyer that her family did not personally know. That time had come so I made up an excuse and went immediately to see the lawyer and file for divorce.

The lawyer I found was an accident lawyer and he told me he did not handle family or divorce types of cases but that they had one of the best divorce lawyers in the country working there. So I set up a meeting to see him but once he found out I was a man trying to get full custody of my children he made up an excuse that he was too busy. So my accident lawyer decided to give it a try with the good divorce lawyer's help. Little did I know the reason I could not find any information on the internet about fathers getting full custody of the children in this state was that it was nonexistent. No father in this state had ever gotten full custody unless the mother did not want the children. The reason the good lawyer did not want the case is because he knew he could not win.

The new lawyer I obtained was a good guy but I could tell he had never had a case like this before and spent a lot of time reading on how to proceed. He did realize that I needed to charge her with child abuse before I divorced her otherwise they might think that I was a disgruntled husband filing for divorce and they would dismiss the child abuse right away. Which meant that I would have to file the child abuse first and then immediately following, file for the divorce. This way I could have her removed from our home and not hurt the children.

I would have to report the abuse in the town where it happened at the child welfare office. How could I be sure though that what happened with the judge was not going to happen at the child welfare office? The truth was, I could not be certain. I would have to take a leap of faith which I did not have at the time. Faith in the system that is, because of course I still had faith in God and I was praying the whole time.

Now, what I am about to tell you really happened but I do not blame you if you do not believe me because I lived it and sometimes I still do not believe it myself. This welfare office was in the middle of town and right next to Martha's new job where she was working as a clerk at the county courthouse. I would have no excuse if I were caught doing this. So I did not call, instead I just stopped and went in to talk to the lady at the office. I told her that I was there to report child abuse. Now I had never been pushed into an office and the door slammed so quick in all my life. I literally thought I was going to jail.

She said, "I know who you are, why would you say something like that out in the middle of the office where someone could hear you?"

"Well," I said, "I was told this is where I was supposed to report it."

She said, "So who is it?" And I told her.

She was a small woman with a very large desk and she peered at me through her thick glasses and told me to come back right at quitting time. She also told me to park out back where no one would see me. She needed to think about this for a while. She quickly ushered me out of the office and told me to leave immediately.

Well, I guess I had just jumped from the frying pan into the fire. I had only been in that office all of five minutes. When I went back to work, I wondered if a swat team would be waiting for me there upon my return. She was obviously scared to be seen with me in her office and I realized that I had not lasted very long trying to save the children. Here I was the first day and already shot down. Suffice it to say, I was a little leery about going back but I knew I had to keep trying.

So I slowly walked in the second time I went there, waiting to be shot down immediately or hauled to jail. The secretary was gone and she was waiting for me with another man whom I had never seen before. I went to walk into the office but he quickly motioned for me to go downstairs which was entirely dark except for the lighted doorway where they wanted me to go. I was nervous going in and was beside myself, unsure of what was going on. I was literally walking into a basement in the dark with people I did not know and no one I knew, knew I was there.

I walked down the dark stairs and into the light. In this office there was another large desk which the lady proceeded to sit behind followed by a large file full of paperwork being thrown on the table. I guess the other guy was the witness to the signing of these documents. Then she asked me while glaring at me through those glasses, "Once you sign these documents there is no going back. I was told to watch for you and if you ever showed up not to give you any help." She paused looked me up and down and said, "You look like a man that's had enough."

I said, "That's me all right.»

Then she told me, "I want you to know just what you are getting into before you do this. The family you will be fighting belongs to what we like to call, 'The Good Old Boys Club'." They are the families that have run this town since before you were born. They do what they please and they control everything from the police and the court system to the schools and the hospitals. Your only saving grace is that I do not like them. You see I have tried to join their club many times over the years and they would never let me in so that is why I am doing this for you now, that and I like kids." Well, she laid it all out for me. She went on to say my only chance was to file these charges and get the government involved because I would have no chance getting help from anyone in this town. Now, more than ever, I realized our chances were slim to none to escape but I had promised the children and I would keep it.

My lawyer had also told me to collect any doctor records as evidence of the abuse. I thought this would be useless but I knew I needed to collect everything I could to win this fight. So I went and got the children's records from all the hospitals, which was tricky since Martha's aunt's work in hospital administration. I had also not realized that the kids had seen so many different doctors in different clinics and when I was done, I had quite a pile in front of me.

As I read the reports I felt sick to my stomach. Report after report of bruises and concussions. Lots of reports I had never known they had even been to the doctor this much. Apparently every time she thought she might have badly injured them she had taken them to the doctor. What else had she kept from me? What else did she not tell me about? There seemed to be some kind of remorse about hitting them and subsequently took them to the hospital to see how badly she had hurt them. I also found out her mother had gone along with her and if the doctor started asking too many questions, she had someone there to back up her story. Great, the woman that was supposed to help the children was actually helping to cover up the abuse. Once the doctor starting questioning all the trips to the hospital Martha, would change clinics and doctors and do it all over again. I had read enough. I now had proof.

After I finally filed the paperwork, all that was left to do was to pick the day. I told the lawyer and the child welfare office that once Martha knew what was happening she would try to hurt the children. Martha's biggest fear is that they would tell and who knows what she might do in retaliation. They needed to remember, she lived by her rules if you hurt me I will hurt you worse. They had decided to have her papers served in person and that she would be notified by the police not to return to the house.

I had to have the papers notarized at the courthouse where my wife worked. So somehow I had to get in and out of the courthouse without anyone seeing me or Martha might find out and that would put the children in more danger. So I decided to do it during the homecoming parade. It would be ideal because Brant, Ann, and Bret were all in the parade on floats. Martha would be at her dad's house with her family waiting to watch the parade. I would have Lily at home with me and if I timed it right I would be waiting at the end of the parade route and pick up the children on the floats. So Lily and I would go to the courthouse and I would get those papers signed and notarized.

If all went according to plan, I would end up at the house with all the children about the time the police were coming to serve Martha the court orders. It had to work out perfectly or the children lives would be at more risk and this plan could easily turn into a horrible mess. So a couple of days before this all happened, I had to let the children in on the plan because it was crucial to its success. Timing was everything in order for us all to end up at our safe zone in the house with the doors locked before Martha got her papers.

After I told them about the plan, I had never before seen them this excited. However, I warned them not to act differently around their mother. We could not allow her to catch on and hurt one or all of them. This unfortunately did not work out entirely as planned. The younger ones followed the rules and did not change their routine but the closer we got to that day the more the older two began to rebel against Martha and tell her just what they thought about her rules. Now the day before the parade I had warned Brant especially, to stay away from Martha because I had never seen her this agitated before she was just waiting for an excuse to hurt someone.

I went to work and had a bad feeling and decided to leave work early. When I got close I could hear the yelling and knew immediately something was worse than normal. I ran to the house and made it to the top of the stairs when I saw it. Martha was punching Brant in the face as hard as she could. I heard the first punch connect before I saw it. It sounded just like on a TV bar fight. The thing that frightened me most was not just the horrible sound of the punch. She was looking in my direction when I got to the top of the stairs and the look on Martha's face was one that still haunts my nightmares. It was pure evil, she was enjoying it, it was a release for her. She wanted to hurt him, kill him, of this there was no doubt. She was using her whole body when she threw those punches. That look of hatred on her face mixed with pleasure made me sick to my stomach. She was enjoying punching Brant in the face over and over again, she needed it. The dragon had been awakened and her snarls of fury sounded demonic as she kept up the beating.

At that moment I knew she would kill him and that hurting the children had become some kind of sick stress release for her. I rounded the top of the stairs as the second punch landed again with a smack and then I was between them trying to hold Martha back as she still tried to get at him while he was running downstairs. It was all I could do to restrain her as she repeatedly yelled at me to get out of the way so she could kill him. Her shrill voice hurt my ears. She was like a wild demon biting and clawing trying to get at Brant.

Then she stepped back and totally under control said, "So you're back early. Your rotten little bastard of a son needed to be taught a lesson and I knew you would not do it so I did." And she calmly walked over to her chair and turned on the television completely satisfied. I could not believe it. This is what happened when I was at work. Had I not come in when I did Brant would surely be dead. Here Martha was now just as calm as could be just seconds after she had tried to bash her sons head in. It made me sick.

I then went downstairs after sending the other children to their rooms and closing their doors. I saw Brant sitting on his bed with a welt raising under his eye and to my surprise he smiled at me through blood stained teeth. He looked at me and said," I guess I showed her, I told her just what I thought of her." His poor body was limp from the attack but he seemed calmer than I had ever seen him.

What could I do but smile back as I sat on his bed next to him and put my arm around him. I said in a calm sickly voice, "You sure did kid, you sure did." The look in his eyes was the look I had been missing. He looked at me like a son should look at his father if he is a good man. It was the soft, warm look of a dog being let in out of the cold. He knew I was on his side and I made a vow to myself that no matter what the cost Martha would never come between us ever again. I did not know it then but two weeks later Brant's two front teeth would fall out because of the punches Martha had given him that day. Later when I asked him if it was worth it he had said, "Oh yeah it was dad, yeah it was."

I made sure he was all right and gave him a frozen bag of peas to put on his eye. I made some food and brought all the children downstairs and we watched a movie where they would be safe for the night. It was all I could do not to give Martha the same beating she had given Brant but tomorrow would be our revenge. My getting in a fight with her now would just end any chance of me getting full custody and I know it made Brant feel better telling her off. He had waited years to tell her what he really thought about her. This had been the release he had been waiting for. All that pent up rage and fear had finally exploded from him. He had slain the beast. After all, he thought he would never see her again after tomorrow. At least, that was the plan. But I knew our chances of winning were like trying to find a needle in a haystack. I vowed to continue doing everything in my power to make this nightmare end. My children were counting on it and the way they looked at me to do it, I could not let them down.

The next day started like any other homecoming day, a lot of running around trying to get the kids everywhere they needed to be. I did not have to see Martha at all that day she because was with her family. Thank God, because after what happened with Brant, it made me sick just to look at her. This was the big day, no turning back after this. For sixteen years I knew this day would come and here it was good or bad it was happening. The stage was set and the pressure was on. I needed help and encouragement, but I also knew the kids and I were on our own. I prayed all night for the strength to get through this.

Brant had come up to me and slapped me on the shoulder and said, "Don't worry Dad you got this." And smiling his winning smile, he went off happier than I had ever seen him, singing a song as he walked to school to find his float for the parade.

That kid always said the right thing when I needed it. There were a lot of things I never told him, like about the judge or the good old boys club. He did not need to know how slim our chances were but I would fix this no matter what. It was my fault I had not given them a good mother. They deserved far better than what they got. I should have picked better but hindsight's twenty-twenty and there was nothing to do now but move ahead no matter how it had to end.

Before I knew it I was running across the parking lot to the back door of the courthouse with my ten-year-old, who was just as frightened as I was about making it in and out without getting caught. There had been nowhere safe to leave her so I had to bring her with me. She understood what was at stake and that getting caught would mean retribution from her mother. I was ashamed that my ten-year-old child should have to be involved in such a thing as this. I had never dreamed we would be here doing this when I got married sixteen years ago.

Before I got out of our Ford Expedition she had seen the worry on my face. Lily grabbed my arm and squeezed herself between me and the steering wheel and put her little hands on both sides of my face and said, "We are not going to get caught everything will be all right. We will stick together and we will win." What could I say to that? I was so proud of her to be so grown up at that age. I felt a little ashamed of my weakness when a ten-year-old kid could be so strong. That was the shot in the arm I needed. With that we raced in signed the papers and raced out. I had never noticed how big the parking lot was. The woman at the window gave us a weird look when she saw the papers we had brought in and I knew we had very little time before Martha would be warned. The lady said she would be served within the hour, just enough time.

We raced to the end of the parade and there were Bret and Ann but where was Brant? He was not where he was supposed to be. Just like always, he was over laughing it up with his friends. I grabbed him and we raced for the pickup and then we were home. I never breathed such a sigh of relief like when I closed the deadbolt from inside the house. Then the phone rang. It was the police they had served the papers and Martha was not allowed to come within a hundred feet of the house. We had done it. It was over. We all let out a sigh of relief, but in the back of my mind I knew it was just the beginning. It would get far worse before it got better and had I known what was about to happen I would have taken the children and ran.

Chapter 12

An End and a Beginning

The children wanted to have a victory party. We had pizza and pop and watched movies all night. I had never seen them this happy. It was hard to believe but at that moment, we were free. No more worry about Martha hurting them and they seemed relieved she was gone, at least for now. As the sun rose on our new freedom another fear arose. A huge weight had been lifted but replaced with a tense unknown. The children and I knew that Martha was all about retaliation. There was no doubt in our minds that she would be waiting for us when we would least expect it. We had foolishly thought that getting her out of the house would reduce our stress. All it had accomplished was a safe zone. Martha could show up anywhere at any time and her mother and father and two sisters would be helping her. It was like being in the water with sharks. We could not see them, but we knew they were there waiting. The children and I had talked about this for a while but there was no way for me to be everywhere at one time. Not only that, but now, the silence was deafening. We had spent so many years with the constant yelling that the silence was unnerving and made the tension even worse. It was so hard for us to talk about being freed from her in our home only to still have her controlling our every move. Would this fear ever end?

We had committed the ultimate sin against Martha by telling the truth about the great secret we had kept for years. We knew that Martha would stop at nothing for retribution. This had been her theme for as long as we had been together and surely she would think our actions were the ultimate betrayal. By Monday we had settled into an uneasy calm and my stomach was tied in knots. All I thought about was getting her out. I had not thought about what would happen next. I had spent years and months planning the escape but what about now. I could trust no one and I soon realized that I could not protect all of the children all of the time.

It had been quiet for a week and then Bret had his last football game. I went alone to watch him knowing that the children were targets every time they left the house. It was a beautiful day and there was the smell of pine in the air from the magnificent pine trees that surrounded the football field. Bret did awesome playing fullback and quarterback in the game. They won their game and I had almost forgotten about our troubles. It was nice to have some peace of mind for a minute.

It really surprised me that Martha had not shown up. At least I did not have to worry about her coming after Bret and ruining his last great game. I was almost to my car when I noticed something out of the corner of my eye. It could not be, Martha and her sisters had been waiting until I left to corner Bret on his way to the bus. They came up trying to hug him and tell him how much they loved him. That was embarrassing enough without everything else going on. They made a huge scene and people were watching. Bret looked like a caged animal that did not know where to run. They had backed him against the grand stand pillar so he could not get away.

I had almost been across the parking lot when I saw what was happening and ran back. I was not sure what to do because they had done this in public and it looked like they had done nothing physical to corner him there. How could I get him out without pushing them out of the way which would land me in jail for sure?

But I could not take them harassing him and his face had turned white as a sheet as he was looking at me to help him.

So I moved in along the stands so as not to touch any one of them. They had not seen me.Bret was still wearing his football gear including his shoulder pads. So I got behind him and pushed him passed Martha and got him onto the bus. Boy were they mad. They were shouting all kinds of obscenities as I walked back to my vehicle making sure not to walk down the road and get run down. I had just gotten to my vehicle when I heard the squeal of brakes right next to me. I had been smart staying out of the road. She had nearly run me down anyway.

Martha was hanging out her car window screaming at me, "You cannot hide the children forever! I will get to them. Just wait and see!" There was no remorse or any inclination that she realized she had just ruined Bret's day and publicly humiliated him. This was all about her and that she had done nothing wrong.

One of Bret's friend's dad was standing by and happened to see what was going on and told me that if I needed him to testify about what had happened in court he would. He said he was sure she would have run me over if a vehicle had not been in the way. He had never seen anything like it in his life and even he was scared, although he was not even close to us. That made me feel better that even bystanders understood how explosive the situation was. Especially when everyone kept saying that it cannot be that bad and how good of a person Martha was. They just did not understand her like I did. She would not stop until she made the children and me pay for telling her wicked secret.

Chapter 13

COURT BEGINS

I found out that there would be two parts to the court hearings. There would be a criminal hearing about the child abuse and the civil trial about the divorce. Once the criminal case started, we would have state protection for the children. But until then and after the criminal trial, it would be up to the local police to protect us. I soon realized that this would be nonexistent because I had acquired a police escort to and from work and it was not the good kind. They made it pretty obvious they were waiting for me to screw up so they could throw me in jail. That is when I realized just what kind of power and influence Martha's family had. The entire police force were either drinking buddies or family friends and that left me out in the cold totally powerless and defenseless.

I also realized how fast the court system worked for those who had friends in high places. Nothing with the private side was supposed to happen until after the criminal hearings. But unfortunately I found out it could if you knew the right people. I was soon in court fighting, not over custody, because she could not get this until after the criminal court was over, but for the visitation rights she wanted. Now, my lawyer was good in the respect that he believed me, but he definitely lacked the experience to deal with this sort of case. Martha had hired a real expensive cut-throat lawyer, which was unexpected. Her family was obviously helping her out.

The first hearing told the story of things to come. I was told to bring Brant and Ann to court as they needed to testify against Martha. This turned out to be a total lie. While we were waiting in the hallway outside of the courtroom, Martha's entire family showed up on the other side of room. Thank goodness the room was large so there was no immediate contact with them. Then the bailiff emerged and escorted me to my seat in the courtroom, although it seemed a little early to me. What did I know, I had never been in court before.

My parents had come along to keep an eye on the children for me. They had sensed the strain I was under from a few phone calls we had and volunteered to be there to help me out. But as soon as the bailiff took me away, Martha's family swarmed Brant and Ann and began trying to hug them and tell them that their mother was really a good person and their father was evil for doing this to get custody. This went on while I was in the courtroom unaware of what was happening outside. My parents had no way to stop them and had no idea what was going on.

I found out later it had all been a trap set up by my father-in-law and the bailiff to get the children in a compromised position where Martha's family could get to them. My father found this out later during the trial because he overheard the bailiff and Dick, my father-in-law, in the back row laughing about how well their plan had worked. The bailiff was a good pal of Dick's and his drinking buddy. Meanwhile Brant ended up in the bathroom throwing up because any contact with Martha made him physically sick. This proved to me that Martha and her family had no regard for the children. They needed to make this "problem" go away and avoid family embarrassment no matter what the cost to the children.

Then the hearing began. During the court hearing Martha was allowed to get on the stand and tell her side of the story while crying and carrying on about missing her children. However, I noticed that I nor the children were asked about how we felt about anything at all. The judge immediately set up a visitation schedule with a counselor present for the initial contact.

Now I had told my lawyer beforehand that the children wanted no contact with Martha and he presented that to the judge. It was as if we were not even there. He expressed deep condolences to my wife for any hardship she was being put through and ordered immediate visitation to begin within the week. Well, this was even worse than expected. How was she being allowed visitation rights immediately with four counts of child abuse waiting in the criminal trial? Not only that, but the judge was telling Martha how sorry they were for her not being able to see her children, that by the way she had beaten for their entire life. This was lunacy. Only now did I realize what I was facing. Not only would the local court back her up but they would also console her through her times of trouble. This should be unlawful! It seemed I was more on trial here than her and what about the children's rights? This was worse than I thought. I at least figured the kids would get their say.

The counseling was to be set up after the court hearing between my lawyer and hers. I had talked to my priest about it too, if the Catholic Church would provide counseling for my children. He said they did not and that we would have to go somewhere else for that. This left me with no options to offer the court for counseling because I did know where else to go. I did not have any idea that all this would happen in the first hearing. If so, I might have been a little more prepared. My lawyer however was putting up a fight after the hearing trying to delay the visitation until after the criminal proceedings, but Martha stepped in and started yelling at him right there in the courthouse.

I felt sorry for him. He got so startled he dropped his briefcase spilling papers everywhere. There is something you need to understand about Martha's yelling. I had heard the term tongue lashing before but had never really understood what it meant until I married Martha. Her voice could bite. It actually caused physical pain in your ears and your very brain to hear it in her angry mood. It was like fingernails on a chalk board. It was booming and shrill and made you jump out of your skin at the sound of it.

She was very proud of it. Of course, you could say it was all in my head, but my lawyer told me after his first engagement with her that she may actually be the spawn of the devil and that he had never heard such a voice like hers ever before. He was very shaken up and expressed his deep condolences for having to live with someone like that for so long. He told me that he could continue to represent me but that maybe I should get someone more used to these specific cases. I think Martha had really scared him.

He tried to find someone else in his firm but no one would take it. However he gave me a list of lawyers who were considered the best for fighting for child's rights. After all, that was what I was fighting for. The children hated her and they were not safe with her. So I made a few calls and hired a new lawyer who was supposed to be a huge advocate for children. There was not enough time to call another hearing so the children would have their first counseling and first visitation with Martha. I could do nothing to stop this now.

As soon as the criminal case ended, she would get visitation unless she was proven guilty by a felony charge at which time she would lose all custody rights to the children. Now we would have to rely on the government to save us because after what I just saw, we had no chance in private court. As far as the children were concerned, Martha would get at least joint custody which is something I would never accept. I would never be able to leave them alone with her so she could enact her hatred upon them.

After the hearing we decided to get out of town for a while and went to stay with my sister who lived in a bigger city about fifty miles away. So we gave a little extra feed and water to the children's little white bunny and left him in the back yard content in his cage. It was the weekend and we all stayed overnight. It was a welcome relief because our home had turned into a prison. We did not feel safe unless the doors and windows were locked and we did not venture outside as we never knew what Martha would do now that the secret was out.

My parents had come and gone and then the children and I ventured back home. Even though there was a protective order for the children, we realized that no matter what she did, the local cops would cover it up. After what we had witnessed at the courthouse she definitely had full cooperation from the courts. As we entered the house, Lily immediately ran out the back door to see their pet bunny. I had barely reached the top of the stairs when Lily came running to me screaming and crying, "Martha killed my bunny! Martha killed my bunny!" I comforted her and told the children to stay inside.

This could not be real. Something else must have happened to the bunny. Surely she did not do this. Martha knew how much that bunny meant to the children. I slowly opened the back door knowing I was not ready to see what was behind it. What I saw was pure horror, not only was the beautiful white bunny dead. Someone had beaten it to death with a club in its cage. Beating it until there was nothing left but hamburger and a little white fur. There was blood and parts of bunny everywhere. You could not even tell what was head or tail.

It made me sick that my youngest daughter had seen her only pet beaten to a pulp. I did not know which was worse the mere sight of it or the fact that she knew her mother did it. Who could do this? What kind of monster could think of this? Not only had she done the deed she knew her children would be the first to see it. If she did this to the bunny who was next? I did not even want to think about it. This was revenge on the children for telling her secret. She had proven again she could hurt them anytime she wanted to.

So much for a protection order. It turned out to be no more than a piece of paper. The dragon had attacked just like we knew she would.

Who would believe this? It was like something on television but here it was happening to us for real. I told the lawyers and anyone else who would listen but they looked at me like I was insane, no one was capable of that, especially Martha. I realized that no one would believe me. I was just the father. In this state I had found out the hard way to say anything against Martha would only hurt our case. So many times I had been told to not say anything by my lawyers. It was better for me to say nothing than to get these looks. The looks that I got from everyone I told about the bunny, were looks like I was absolutely nuts. Even the people who thought I was telling the truth did not want to believe it. They did not want to believe it because it would keep them up at night that such pure evil exists. It was just a lot easier to label me as a vindictive father than to face the truth. This was a message sent to the children from Martha that they were not safe anywhere, she was always watching. It made me sick cleaning up that mess and after I was done we had a funeral for the bunny up on the hill in the backyard. She could not hurt him anymore. We did not sleep that night who could after that.

Brant had still been running cross country and had been doing well that year. In fact, he qualified for state the previous two years but just barely and this year, he was running much faster. He was a shoe-in for state. But all this trouble with Martha made him physically sick. After the hearing Brant had only three days before cross country regions, he could not eat a thing until finally the night before the big meet he ate a can of chicken noodle soup. I had told him he needed to skip the race that he was in no shape to run. The poor kid was skinny to start with and now he looked like a skeleton with skin stretched over it. Brant would have none of it because to him skipping the race meant Martha won. He would have run that race even if it killed him. The day of the race finally came and I nearly had to carry him to the starting line. I asked him one more time if he was sure he wanted to do this. Brant said, "She will not beat me this time."

Then bang went the gun and they were off. It was something to watch all the colors of the different schools against the green of the golf course. I had to say it. I was scared for him. On a good day a cross country race was hard and as sick as Brant was, I just hoped I would not have to take him to the hospital. He was running his heart out and just out of placing on the last curve. I was trying to tell him where he was so he knew how many he had to beat to place. The top twenty got to go to state and as I counted them coming in, it was close. I counted nineteen, twenty, and aww he just missed placing by one runner. He was twenty-first. I had been taping his race with my camcorder and I swore, one of the only times in my life that I swore, and it is caught on tape. He did not deserve this. But it was good thing I could not count because he turned out to be number twenty after all and qualified for state! He did it with one can of soup. I carried him off the green this time. His legs looked like noodles and he was a limp as a leaf but he had done it. After a second or two on the ground, he dragged himself to his feet, holding onto the pole at the finish line and shook the hand of every runner as they finished. It was a tradition he had at every race. I was so proud of that skinny kid showing such good sportsmanship in a world that had gone out of its way to crush him. Martha would not win this time.

He would run at the state competitions a week later and place in the top fifty with his best time ever. He could not be stopped. When Brant wanted something, he went for it. No matter the odds. Try to tell him he could not do something and he would. If we could survive getting away from Martha, Brant's potential would be limitless.

Lily would have her birthday next and I was very worried. We did have child protection and I had provided the school with paperwork that Martha could not see the children without court-ordered supervision. I thought that would be enough. I sent the children to school and headed to work that day. I was really surprised when I received a phone call to come pick up Lily she was crying and would not stop. When I reached the school she immediately ran up to me and jumped into my arms.

The principal explained that Martha showed up to see Lily. After asking Lily three times to see if she wanted to see her mother. Lily had abruptly said no. However the principal said that Martha had been very persistent and he had gotten scared because she was yelling at him. So the principal tricked Lily into coming into a room at which point Martha came in and locked the door so Lily could not get away so she could tell her happy birthday.

I could not believe it. Here was Lily in a public school and Martha was able to walk right through a court order and instead of them protecting Lily, they lied to her and locked her in a room with the one person she was most scared of in the whole world. Now what? We need to add schools as another place the children were not safe? The principal begged for forgiveness evidently feeling bad because of Lily's reaction. I said the only forgiveness I would have is if he protects Lily from now on. He said he would but could I believe him? I doubted that.

I also found out later from Lily that Dick, her grandfather, showed up at the bus stop to give Lily a birthday card. When she refused to take it Dick chased Lily round and round the bus at a busy intersection trying to give her a hug until she got on the bus and hid. I could not believe it, what if a car hit her? This was way out of hand. Who would I report it to, the cops? They would only laugh just like the last time I tried to report something to them. I told my lawyer but there was nothing he could do. If the police were unwilling to make a report that was the end of it.

While Lily told me the story, she was so very proud that she had escaped Dick and hid from him. What could I say but, "Good job" and gave her a hug. She was the only one who had acted like

Chapter 14

VISITATION

After the court hearing I had to tell the children the news. News that would be sadder than death. They would have to see Martha. After what happened to the bunny they did not want to see her at all of course. Sadly, it had taken even less time than I thought for my promise to them about not seeing their mother to be broken.

Their first thoughts were to run away. None of the kids wanted to ever see or hear from her again. They did not miss her at all and finally felt safe at home because she was gone. They did not understand why they had to see her if they did not want to. Not only that but they were utterly scared of her. They told on her and now she would get them back. The bunny incident proved that.

The children thought that the judge must be on her side. After all, no one asked them how they felt about it. What could I tell them? I could not believe it either that someone with a child abuse case pending could be granted visitation so easily with the very children she was accused of beating. So I decided to tell the children what the courts had told me. They had told me that they would put me in jail and custody would be taken away from me and that I had no choice about it. Another way to get rid of me. Instead they would force me to bring the children to Martha where she could get to them. Did my children have no rights at all? In my mind they were more grown up than Martha in so many ways and yet their voices were not even taken into account. They were not even asked about their fate. What a world to live in where the victim is guilty until proven innocent.

We were sent to Lutheran Social Services for counseling and not only did I have to take the children there but I also had to pay for it. This is where the visitation would take place. The children and I were supposed to meet the counselor there. I had been told by everyone that counseling would help them a lot. I was not very impressed with the place. The building looked to be condemned and the counselor's office was in a back corner barely big enough for all of us to fit in. The furniture looked like leftovers from a rummage sale. The gloominess of the office did nothing to lift our spirits.

The counselor had met earlier that day with Martha and would meet with us tonight and tomorrow before their first visitation together. I had seen the children's faces and I knew that seeing Martha was only going to hurt them. They were extremely afraid of her and I thought they might run away to avoid her. The counselor seemed to be sure that a supervised visit would greatly empower the children and help them out immensely. She told me that the children needed to be able to confront their mother in a safe place so they could express their feelings toward her without fear of retaliation. She seemed overly excited about the visitation and what really confused me is that she did not ask the children any questions regarding it. Ann being the outspoken one told her they wanted nothing to do with Martha but the counselor talked over her and ignored her completely.

When I asked her what would happen if I refused to bring them, she got very quiet. For the record, she was a huge woman, about six foot four inches and three hundred and fifty pounds. She stood up behind her little desk and waved her somewhat large finger at me and said that would be a huge mistake and that she would have me arrested for that. I simply asked this question so the children could see that I was not lying to them. She dismissed the children and I expressed my concerns that the children had no interest in seeing their mother and that they were extremely afraid of what she might do to them. She looked at me unbelievingly and said, "You should not pretend to be protecting the children when we all know better and I will repeat this, it will be wonderful for the children to see their mother it will help them immensely. I will swear out a warrant for your arrest if you are not here promptly at eight o'clock."

I could tell she really did not like me but then I did not think much of her either. I had the feeling this was not going to help the children at all. But either I bring them or go to jail and then Martha could get full custody which is exactly what she wanted to happen. It seemed that the counselor and Martha had already decided how this visitation would go and there was absolutely nothing I could do about it.

That night was quiet as death at our house for tomorrow the kids would have to see their mother and we all knew how this would turn out. Unfortunately there was nothing we could do now but play it out and so we did. The trip was like a funeral procession. The silence in the car was deafening as we proceeded to the meeting. I looked in my rear view mirror and there was the old familiar sight of the cop car that was my own personal shadow always lurking behind me waiting, just waiting for me to try to run for it. I was almost sure they already had the warrant for my arrest made out sitting on a desk somewhere.

Brant had already told me of his plan to get through the counseling. After all, the last time he had seen her had made him physically sick. Brant wore glasses since a young age. They were as thick as pop bottles and without them he could barely make out faces. He had decided that the only way to endure a meeting with her was to leave his glasses at home. This seemed to be a great idea to me. How could these kids, after all they had been through, be put through such a horrible ordeal? He was not going to wear his glasses because he could not even stand to see her. Where was the justice?

Martha was already there when we got there. The children would not move. It was as if they were super-glued to their seats. Brant looked at me and said, "Are you sure we cannot run?"

I said, "We would not get far," pointing behind me to the police car that had just parked across the street. We went in and the run down building made none of us feel better about it. The counselor met us outside and told me I had to stay in the waiting room. I said, "Are you absolutely sure they will be safe in there?"

The counselor shrugged her shoulders and said, "Sure why not?" and with a huff shuffled the children in. It seemed forever that hour dragged by like the last hours of one's life. There was an old worn bible sitting on the table that by the layer of dust on it had not been opened for a long time. I sat and read the bible hoping and praying that this would not turn out as bad as I thought it would. The minutes ticked by as if each minute was pounding in my brain all the while thinking how I had failed them. Everything had gone her way and now here we were and she was fulfilling her promise that she could get to them anytime she wanted to. As the minutes ticked by the Bible bent in my hands as if I were holding on to it for dear life. Then it was over and on the old worn cover of the Bible were my fingerprints where I had held on for my children. The pain I had felt for them seemed to have rocked me to my very soul and I felt totally worn and used by the time the hour was up.

The counselor came out just glowing and went over to me and told me how well the consultation had gone and that the children were so happy to see their mother. I looked at her like she was an alien and wondered if she had gotten her degree out of a cereal box. She said for Martha's safety that I would have to leave the room and stay in the closet until she was safely in her car because she felt threatened by me. When I refused she wanted to know if she had to involve the police in this matter. There it was again, treating me like a criminal when all I wanted was to protect my children. I had never been threatened so much with jail time in my entire life just for trying to protect my children.

I had been calm through this entire event and here the counselor was looking for any reason to throw me in jail. I guess I was really the one on trial, not my loving wife who could make tears appear out of midair. So I hid in the closet while Martha made her way out of the building. Once I was let out of the closet the children looked worse than I had even feared. They were almost transparent white and looked like someone had killed their favorite pet. Oh wait Martha did do that. I looked at the counselor and I stated, "The children do not look happy. They look more like the walking dead. I thought you said it would empower them. Just what happened in there?" She stated that it had all gone according to plan and that I would see the progress later.

I wanted to tell her off. I could see from the expressions on the children's faces that something had gone terribly wrong in there. They were all staring at their feet like they did when Martha punished them. They said not a word as they filed out of the dreary building into the car. After we had gotten in the car and was driving down the road I asked them what had happened.

There was nothing but stunned silence until Ann said, "The counselor let Martha run the whole meeting and she backed her up. Martha started yelling at us and when we tried to stop her or tried to ignore her the counselor spoke up and defended her by telling us we needed to respect our mother and listen to her. We were not empowered like the counselor said it was just like we were back home with her and she got to do just what she wanted. She even pulled Brant up to her face and made him look her in the eye while she chewed him out for saying bad things about her."

I was stunned I knew it would be bad, but this, this was worse that the counselor had not only not let the children have their say, but had backed up Martha and actually let her carry out her abuse in the meeting. Either the counselor was totally stupid or she thought nothing had actually happened. The counselor had done none of the things in the meeting she had told me about and had instead demoralized the children by making them obey Martha's every whim. Even making Brant look her in the eye which is what she had always done before she hit him.

This whole incident made me sick to my stomach. Not only had it made the children way worse off than before by making them feel that they had done something wrong. The counselor had solidified this by backing Martha up. After this experience, counseling would never be a viable solution to talk their problems out. This first initial contact had destroyed any possible relationship they might have with any counselor. Now counselors would be added to the list of police, judges, and bailiffs as people who would not believe them and could not be trusted.

The ride home was silent. I did not even have a clue what to say to them and I had totally failed to protect them. The justice system had not only destroyed their chances to get away from their mother but it had also rendered them silent so that the blame for their lost innocence and the beatings were all their fault. After all, all the grown- ups had told them that they were wrong and Martha was right; if not verbally to their faces, then inadvertently by their actions. This was worse than I thought. We had lost and not only that, but the court system and now the counselor who was supposed to be looking at this from a neutral standpoint had joined Martha's side without hearing the children at all. I might even lose custody the way this was playing out.

We got home and I assured them that it was not their fault and Martha was to blame. According to the court I was not supposed to speak badly about Martha to the children but I did not care. It was us against all of them and I needed to show the children that at least I knew the truth and would back them up when they needed it. She should not have hurt them no matter what they did. Though most the time it was for no reason at all. I was not supposed to do this but I was not going to let them think they were in this alone. I figured if they did not have to play by the rules than neither did I. They were just children and to have so many adults tell them they were wrong and that they deserved all those beatings was worse than wrong, it was immoral.

I put them to bed. I looked down at their white drawn sickly faces and tucked them in and gave each a kiss on the forehead and told them that I loved each of them. Now what was I to do? This was like some bad nightmare that would not end and just kept getting worse. So much for doing this the legal way. It had been a mistake to think the children could get justice. But what was to happen next would be far worse than anything we had faced so far.

Chapter 15
THE E.R.

The next morning Brant could still not tell me how he felt. He was lethargic to say the least. The boy who always had a smile on his face was now a shade of green. He would barely say anything at all and could not get out of bed. I had to go to work because I had missed too much already and my boss was asking questions and hinting I had better not miss any more. So I left Brant in bed and got the others to school even though they should not have gone. They were not feeling much better than Brant. They were barely functioning. I dropped them off and headed to work and as I drove I felt a mounting fear like I had never felt before.

I had decided to call Brant from work. I had left the phone right on his bed so he could reach it if he had to. It was a long ride to work. I had finally gotten there and I called home. It rang and rang and then a feeble voice answered and I asked, "How are you doing buddy?"

He slowly said, "I don't know." That was it, I told the secretary that I was leaving for a medical emergency and to tell the boss when he came in. I had read enough to know that with depression if a person could not answer how they feel that they needed help immediately. I had done a lot of reading about mental health in trying to deal with Martha. When I was trying to find something to help her. Also when the children started counseling so that I could help them the best that I could. Something was wrong, very wrong. I needed to get him and the others medical help. Brant had never sounded like this before and there had to be something wrong for him to answer like that.

The other children were just as I had left them pasty white and incoherent like they had taken a break and did not want to come back. Who could blame them after everything they had been through. I picked them up and met Brant at home then I called the hospital to see their regular doctor. She had always been very good with the children. I called and my call was sent immediately to the doctor which I thought was strange. Dr. Kinder, the children's physician answered, "What can I do for you?"

I told her that I needed an appointment for her to see my four children. The phone immediately went quiet and she said she could not see them today at any time. This was strange as we had never not been able to get in to see her when we called, not ever. Then I asked if any other doctor had any openings today and she said no and that if I wanted help we would have to go to the Emergency Room. This was absurd! It is a small hospital and there was always someone around especially on a weekday.

Then it dawned on me Martha's aunt was on the hospital board. I had long since given up on coincidence and I was sure they had blackballed us. This made me sick that Martha's whole family was a bunch of loathsome animals not even allowing the children to get medical attention. So I took all four children who were already having one of the worse days of their lives to an ER which is not fun even for an adult. All because of a family that wanted to destroy four little kids for telling the truth.

We got to the ER and thank God we got a doctor from the big city fifty miles away. Now maybe he could help the children. The doctor, Dr. Goodwin, a young man of about thirty-five came in. He was very business-like as I explained what happened. He seemed very concerned and brought out his nurses and met with each child to assess what was going on with each one by themselves in a closed room.

After it was over he told me that each child had told him very similar stories about their meeting with Martha. Dr. Goodwin had diagnosed all the children with P.T.S.D, which stands for Post-Traumatic Stress Disorder. I was very confused and asked him if this was the same as what soldiers in war are often diagnosed with. He told me yes, but it is also a diagnosis for anyone who has gone through traumatic experiences, child abuse counts. I was floored by this. This explains why they appeared so lethargic.

He also told me that they were all in bad shape but that Brant needed to be seen by the psychiatrist at the ER in the city that night to be evaluated and possibly admitted into the child suicide watch ward there immediately. He said I could drive him and the meeting had already been set up. He added that it needed to be done right away because Brant was in very bad shape. The doctor told me that in Brant's mental state it was impossible for him to tell if he was suicidal or not and that every precaution must be taken to make sure he would not hurt himself. Brant had not said he wanted to kill himself but could not say how he felt and this was very serious indeed.

Then he also added that they took child abuse very seriously at the hospital in the big city and that he needed to have this documented by a law enforcement officer and that it was mandatory in a case such as this. Here we go I thought to myself, but did not say anything to the doctor but "good luck," which made him give me a quizzical look. He would find out I thought but maybe this time it would be different. Maybe the police here would actually follow the law, but I did not hold my breath.

Sure enough the doctor returned with a puzzled look to me as he held the phone, he said, "They would like to talk to you," with a tone that suggested this was highly out of the ordinary.

I answered, "Hello." What followed came from the chief of police.

He said in a rather sarcastic tone, "I heard what the doctor had to say in this matter but I find no reason that this or any other complaint from you or your children would warrant any documentation by us or that we should get involved at all." And then click, he hung up.

The doctor looked dumbfounded, "I have never had the police totally neglect a child abuse case like this. It is absurd. What do you think I should do about it?" as he threw up his hands and looked directly at me like I should be mad about it. I think he thought I should have some logical explanation for what just happened.

I said, "Since I filed this lawsuit against my wife for child abuse, for which you just took statements from my children and now know how grave it is, the police have totally abandoned us. Not only that, but they follow me around waiting for me to make a mistake and today you are the only doctor in this entire hospital that would even see the children because my wife and her family said we could not be seen here. I am maddened by these circumstances but there is absolutely nothing that you or I can do about it."

He then looked at me with pity in his eyes and began to apologize that he could do no more and he just kept saying how he had never seen or heard of anything like this before. Before this was over, I would hear this same thing over and over again and no one, I mean no one could tell me what to do about it. So off to city. I would go to my sister's to drop off three kids who had just spent four hours in an ER talking to complete strangers about things they just wanted to forget. I would be taking Brant to the psychiatrist, which was about to be the hardest thing up to this point that I would ever have to do. All because of a broken court system, an evil woman and her family, and an idiot therapist.

I knew where we were going and I would have to choose, because of these people, the one situation I had been desperately trying to avoid. I would have to choose to have locked up, the boy who held the doors at church and had been an inspiration to others, in a psychiatric institution to be put on suicide watch because his mother had pushed him too far. I had told them, all of them, and they had ignored me and acted like it was some stupid game they were playing. This was life and death for the most important people in my life, my children, and they had laughed. Martha had her revenge. She had used the system to destroy her oldest son and caused great damage to the other children all because they had told the truth.

In that fifty miles to the hospital, I counted ten giant bill boards that stated phone numbers for turning in child abuse and that it was against the law and your civic duty to do so. This was child abuse awareness month and I had seen many ads on television. It made me sick. What an ironic and horrific joke this was. We had done the right things. I had tried to save my children from a hideous monster but instead, had made everything worse. I had shown them what it was like without her in our home and it was wonderful. Now it was over and the courts were making sure she received everything she wanted and the children got nothing but more heartache and grief.

They lived in the prison that was our home while Martha went around raising havoc in their lives when and where she pleased. Their accusations backed up by facts had been thrown in their faces and treated like lies and they were rebuked for telling them. Now it was me who would have to make this horrific choice caused by people who did not even know Brant. The sweet good boy who would have to be locked up because the government and the system had not only not provided justice but had given Martha her chance to enact her vengeance upon them. She had done this in counseling of all places.

I dropped the other children off with my sister telling them I would be back soon. They had developed a dependence on me to be there so they would feel safe because at this point they did not trust anyone else. It was already the middle of the night somewhere around eleven o'clock when we entered the ER This was no place for a young boy especially after the night and day he had just had. I half carried, half guided him to a seat and told them we were here to see Dr. Wainwright the psychiatrist on call. We still ended up waiting an hour for him to get there since the psychiatric ward was across town. I had never known a night to be so black, so unforgiving, as that night.

All that time I was hoping he would prescribe drugs or an overnight stay but looking at Brant lying there on my shoulder he needed more than that. We were finally admitted and the giant pile of paperwork was done and the doctor needed to talk to Brant alone. I sat in the waiting room praying to know the right thing to do next. I had never been in this kind of a situation. What was I supposed to do? I had tried so hard not to end up here in this place. I could see the writing on the wall. I knew my children could take no more, but did anyone listen, no.

I was worn out and thinking. Why should Brant have to pay the price? Hadn't he paid enough for an abusive mother who never loved him nor showed love his whole life? Then the doctor came out and it was my turn to go in while a nurse stayed with Brant. I did not know what to expect but what came next was as bad as I had thought. The doctor verified that Brant had PTSD since Brant could not evaluate his own feelings, Dr. Wainwright advised me that he needed to be admitted to a lockdown facility and put on suicide watch for his own safety.

I asked if I could get him out since I am admitting him. The doctor told me what I was afraid of, that he could only be released if the doctors said he could go. That was it then. I would have to decide my beautiful boy's entire life here and now in an instant. I would be committing him to life in prison essentially by signing this paperwork. There was only me here to make this decision.

I cursed the court system, my evil wife, and everyone else involved. They should have to pay the price not him. What if I took him home and he did commit suicide? I could not live with that. So I asked for a moment with Brant and I put my arm around him. I asked him, "So do you know what is going on."

Brant said, "They want to lock me up."

I said in a rather small voice, "You are right."

Then Brant asked, "Can Martha come see me?"

I said, "No, no she cannot."

Then Brant said in a voice as hard as rock, "Then have them lock me up dad."

It was the bravest thing I had ever seen. He was willing to sacrifice his freedom to get away from her. Those idiots needed to be here now and see this brave unwavering boy go to prison so he could be safe from his abusive mother. So I signed the papers and with each stroke of the pen I felt the noose tighten around my throat. How would we come back from this? Where was the path, all I could see was the darkness closing in on us. Brant was the light. He was the boy who could do anything. How could we win by locking away the light?

In the middle of the night my son was stripped of his clothing, even his shoes because on suicide lockdown they could not have anything on that they could use to hurt themselves. Dressed in a loose hospital gown and slippers my son was loaded onto a transportation truck with two armed guards. I asked them if he could have a coat but they would not let him have one. It was the dead of winter and very cold out. I thought they could at least give him a coat.

I followed them in the freezing rain in the early morning to the lockdown facility. I was allowed to follow to see where he was and tell him goodbye. When we arrived I found out it was indeed a locked down facility. There were adults on the first floor and teenagers and children on the second floor. I was escorted by a guard and told to say goodbye at the electric doors. I gave Brant a long hug and said, "I am sorry son."

Brant looked up at me and said, "Don't worry dad. I'm safe now." And with that, the doors closed. I got outside the door and headed to my car as the tears began to fall. We lost. Martha won. She got her revenge.

I had to call the so-called therapist because the children had another supervised visitation set up for the next day and I told her she needed to call it off because of what had happened with Brant. She tried to say it was all in my head until she heard what facility Brant was in. Then she clammed up and cancelled everything until we could have another hearing. Maybe Brant won after all, only time would tell.

Chapter 16

GRAND JURY

My parents arrived and we all stayed at my sister's place on the weekend and returned home after to keep the kids in school and so I could make some money to keep the lights on. Having my parents there, especially my dad, made me feel better. It was like having backup instead of standing alone. My father was always the rock that I could count on and it was nice to know I was not crazy with so many people telling me I was.

Ann, Bret, Lily and I ventured home again with my parents. I had left a key for the house with my next door neighbor and had her keep an eye on things when we were gone. She had always been my friend since we moved in and had watched Lily for me several times after school. She thought the world of Lily and we really liked her too. She was one of the few people in town I could still trust. I found out how very few friends I had after I kicked Martha out.

But as I turned into the driveway I knew something was wrong. My neighbor came running out to meet me. She told me that Martha and the police had been to the house. She told me the police had threatened and forced her to give them the extra key she had and had gone into the house. How could this be? There was a protection order that she could not come within a hundred feet of the house. Yet somehow Martha had the police come with her and break the law. I was furious but what was worse is that she had taken things from the house.

I did not care if she took stuff but I was not even notified and how did they know we were not home. Martha must have known about Brant. So while I had to have our son admitted into a lockdown psychiatric ward, she meanwhile had broken into our home with the police and cleaned us out! She had not only taken her things but the children's things as well. She took their photos, medals, and keepsakes that they loved. She even took their piggy banks. I was floored.

I was furious and called the police station. My neighbor, who was extremely upset by this whole episode, told me the police officer's name. I demanded to talk to him to find out just how this could happen and have him explain it to me. The policeman answered and with a smug condescending tone replied, "It is her house too. She had every right to take her things."

I replied trying to keep my cool, "What about the children's things she took. For God's sake she even took their piggy banks."

The policeman smirked, "Whatever she took was hers."

My anger with mounting with every word this smug S.O.B. was saying and now he was laughing at me. He did not care one bit about anything I had to say. Then I lost it and yelled, "You know you helped her break the law by letting her in!"

He replied in a demeaning voice, "Who are you going to report it to. We make the law around here," then I heard a click; he had hung up. This is exactly what I had known from the beginning. The entire police force was just waiting for me to screw up. Martha could do anything she wanted including stealing little kid's piggy bank money and the cops would back her up.

What was I supposed to do now? Now we knew for a fact we were not safe in the house. First, the bunny incident and now this. This is with a protection order in place. What will happen when we lose it? I could not report it to the police they would not even hear it. I called my lawyer to see what to do. She told me that if the police would not file a report that I should lay low and say nothing. There was nothing else to do.

Did I have any rights? Did the children have any rights? I had just had my son institutionalized and now we had been robbed and there was no one to tell. Actually the only one being threatened with jail time was me. How could this possibly make sense? It was an impossible situation.

We went to visit Brant every day and he was doing well in there. He, of course, had made many new friends because the floor was full of teenagers. Most of whom were abused and felt safer in there than at home. The forgotten children; that is what they were, just normal everyday kids in very abnormal living environments and Brant found he had a lot in common with them.

He felt a lot better knowing Martha was out there and he was in here, which in and of itself was wrong on so many levels. Martha should have been the one locked up so Brant could go on living his life. I never saw anyone come to visit any of the other children in the ward the entire time we were there and I never missed visiting hours to spend time with Brant. It was a very sad place. It was an all-white walled facility, as if that could hide the pain in these walls. These were the lost children thrown away by our society. My children had at least me fighting for them. These children had no one. I never saw anyone show up for any of them. What chance did any of them have? If I was having this kind of trouble trying to save my own kids from a monster, all these children ever had were monsters in their lives. They had no chance at all with no one fighting for them. A child's voice means nothing in our court system. Through these walls I could hear the silent screams of abuse and neglect and our legal system had nothing but deaf ears for them, the forgotten children.

When I visited, we played a lot of pinnacle and board games which Brant really liked. The only disturbing thing, other than the guards and the whole lockdown situation, was that Brant's bunk mate continually talked about killing himself and harming others which kept all of us on edge especially Brant. It was depressing to see so many young people with nowhere to go and no one looking out for them. I had never believed we would be here when this all started but the system had given us the boot. We were down for the count but that did not mean we would give up. There was still fight left in us.

Meanwhile during all this, the criminal case was moving forward which moved like an ant in the wintertime compared to the private sector. Certain people did not want this to go to court so of course it was put on the back burner. Our prosecuting attorney was a likable family man and at first thought he would do a bang up job for us. He talked a lot about justice and doing what was right but I would soon find out he was like all the rest just trying to sweep us under the rug.

I had of course found all those documents from the different hospitals confirming the children's frequent trips to the doctor and ERs, which in my mind should have been plenty to put Martha away. It was a lot of evidence especially with identical accounts from the children of the incidents in question. There were over ten with corroborating evidence from the doctor visits to confirm their stories.

Everything from stitches to large bruises, and when questioned by the doctor, Martha would promptly switch to another doctor as to avoid any further questioning. I worked a lot of hours and she took care of all the doctoring and bills so I did not even know about many of these instances. That is when I realized just how good of an actress she was, some of these doctor reports went back fourteen years. Fourteen years she had gotten away with this abuse of her own children. What baffled me more was that she was a preschool teacher and I had seen her around other children. She was sickly sweet and affectionate to other children just not her own. Beating and starving our children had been her release which made her somehow feel better about herself to cope with the world. The more I found out the less I could understand it.

Now back to the criminal case. We had started out with four counts of child abuse with corroborating evidence from multiple doctors notes from two different hospitals. It was one week from the grand jury trial, during which time the visitation had happened. Brant was now in the psych ward in the city when the prosecutor told my father and I in a meeting that he would only be pursuing three counts of simple assault against Martha and not the original four counts of child abuse.

From the beginning, we were issued a Diplomatic Security Service (DSS) investigator and a court liaison for the criminal hearings to walk us through the process. The investigator had interviewed each child at school so no bias could be seen in the interviews. Each child verified the exact same accounts of multiple incidents at our home; from Martha throwing objects that hit the child hard enough for several stitches, to slamming them in a large sliding door on the van, to pushing them down a fifteen-foot flight of stairs kicking them as they went down to the point where the other children had to pull the one she was attacking into another room to stop the attack.

Each of these things had happened multiple times so these were no accidents and each child said as much. They did not tell me about it because Martha had convinced them that I knew all about it and it would get much worse if they told. As I said she was a very good actress and never left me alone with the children, which was the key. If she had, we might have figured it out if we were able to have had the chance to talk amongst ourselves. But she had used us against each other with a very elaborate set of lies with the intent of tearing us apart. This had been her dark sinister plan for our family for years. What a truly evil person to put so much work into destroying her own children.

Anyway, it floored me that the prosecutor was not going to follow up the suit as child abuse and I asked him as much. The prosecutor told me that no jury in this state would convict a woman of child abuse. It just did not happen. He tried to convince me that this was our only chance of convicting her of anything because a mother in this state had all the rights and fathers were never given even partial custody. So he told me that I was very lucky that I had full custody now because it just was not done. He literally admitted that if we were in any of the four states bordering this state that I would have been given permanent full custody already but in our backwoods backwater of a state, it was not done. I had never been so ashamed or trapped by the state I lived in.

I told him, "But what about all the evidence and testimony by the children. They had told me in the beginning that the odds of four children this young having the same stories was near impossible." Yet my children had given them exactly that! Four near identical accounts of multiple incidents of abuse. My father and I argued with him till we were blue in the face but he would not do anything but the simple assault charges.

I told him that I needed a felony conviction so she would lose her chance for custody because by all accounts if she was not convicted in criminal court, the private sector would at least give her partial custody. The prosecutor said not to worry. If she is convicted of all three misdemeanors then it would count as a felony and she would lose custody anyway. This was something, but what were the odds of getting all three convictions?

I said just add one case of child abuse in case the grand jury wanted to prosecute her. The prosecutor looked at me and said, "They will put your children on the stand and tear them apart. Is that what you really want? I thought your son was already in a psych ward in the city. Do you honestly want the rest of them there too? Believe me I know what I am doing."

So with no fighting points left, I put my children's fate in the hands of this prosecutor and the state to do the right thing. To be honest at this point I had little to no faith in the court system and absolutely no one had asked the children what they wanted. According to everyone else only Martha's opinion counted.

The day had finally come to testify before the grand jury. My daughter Ann had decided to testify against her mother since Brant was in no condition to testify. It was the bravest thing I had ever seen. To see a fifteen year old girl testify against the monster that was her mother to have her locked up where she could never hurt any of them again. Ann had realized that she was the only one of the children who could provide a voice for herself and her brothers and sister.

Besides that, the awful trip to the counselor and what Martha had done to Brant had made her so mad that she did not care who heard the story. She just needed to tell it. So there we were in a basement hallway of the very courthouse where my wife worked. Indeed she was right above us on the second floor. It was me, Ann, my mom and dad, the court liaison, and the DSS investigator waiting to see a bunch of strangers and tell them the story that will ultimately decide our fate.

The minutes slowly ticked by and I looked at the liaison and investigator who I knew were staying neutral, just doing a very difficult job, and asked them, "How many times in all your cases have you seen a father get full custody in this state?" Neither answered, but from the look on their faces, they did not have to. I had never met anyone who told me we had a chance anyway, especially in this state. There were some things in this world of chaos that were helpful and that was our DSS liaison and investigator. They explained everything they could and we felt safe when they were around. They were the only ones in this court system that made us feel that way. We are grateful to them.

The process for our testimony was for us to wait in a long hallway until the grand jury was ready for us. First Ann would be called into the room at the end of the hallway. I would not be allowed to enter with her. Only the prosecutor, who at this time, I did not trust. Then Ann would exit and I would be called in to give my testimony. It was a simple plan in the enemy's lair. The last time we were here, they, and the system, had walked all over us.

They called Ann in. Again she would tell her story. How many times was this? I had lost count. It did not seem to matter because no one wanted to listen anyway and the odds of us winning this was near impossible. We needed Martha found guilty on all three counts for it to help us or it would be back to the private sector we go. Back to the crying Martha show and I already knew what would happen there. This was it our last chance. Everything hung on them, the jury. God help us. There was no one else who could or would help at this point.

Ann came out of the grand jury room on a run like she could not get out fast enough. Her long blonde hair flying in the air and a look of release on her face. She told them and now her job was done. I saw the worry lines on her round little face and thought she looked too old for her age. Her life had been too hard for too long. Now it was my turn. I entered the room. The room was small and cramped and I was sure this was not the usual room where they held these meetings. There we were in the basement again, just like always, where we could not be seen. It was very intimidating to have a full jury staring at you. At that moment I thought of my daughter who had just given her testimony. It seemed that the children were guilty of some crime by the way they had been treated. I sat in the chair next to the prosecutor and the questioning began.

The same questions that we had answered so many times but I found I could not look them in the eye. Over half the jury were women, every age, every size. The entire group seemed to hang on every word and their inadvertent gaze shrunk me until I seemed to be an inch tall. My face felt flushed and my throat felt dry like I was choking as I told our story. I could not even imagine how it had been for the children telling this same story over and over to complete strangers. It was like a living nightmare.

Then the questioning was over and the jury gathered to the back of the room to deliberate. I heard raised voices in unison and then the leader, a small stately woman, the picture of what a grandmother should look like, walked forward and eyed the prosecutor like a piece of meat. She looked like a bandy chicken, which is a little chicken that will fight anything no matter the size, looking for a fight. "We the jurors would like to know if we can bring forward more charges of child abuse against Martha. We do not feel that these charges are enough."

If ever I wanted to strangle someone at that moment, it was that prosecutor. For all his talk that they would never prosecute her for child abuse. This jury wanted to file their own charges against Martha for what she had done. They would have found her guilty of all charges we could have put against her. Instead the prosecutor replied, "No you can only reply to the charges put before you." At this there was a groan from the group, more like a boo.

You could tell the jury was mad. In their faces was a look of disgust, whereas if Martha would have been there, she would not have made it out of the room. Then the leader stepped forward and said, "Then it is unanimous. We, the jury, find her guilty of all three counts of simple assault." It was over! We got justice and yet, had gotten none. The people had thrown the book at her but the government would not allow it. The prosecutor said nothing and disappeared like the wind. I am sure the look I gave him when she asked for more charges threw the fear of God into him.

Well, I thought at least I would not have to face her in private court again. We had won a little victory thanks to regular people. They actually listened to the victims for the first time since this all started. It felt good that they listened and convicted her. It was not all in our heads and decent everyday people like us unanimously felt the same.

Now we could finally start over. Martha could not even get visitation rights with this felony count against her, let alone custody. I had one final meeting with the prosecutor before it was over. I entered his office, thankful that it would be the last time, and the world can go back to normal again.

The prosecutor was overjoyed when I entered the room as he told me Martha had pleaded guilty to two of the three counts of simple assault and she would serve two weeks in jail. I was stunned and said, "What are you talking about? We needed all three counts for her to lose her parental rights."

The prosecutor said, "They pleaded out or they would have put your kids on the stand and tore them apart."

I answered, "You fool they would have put her away if it was not for you! Now I will have to fight her in private court where I have no chance." He simply shrugged his shoulders as if I should have been happy with what he had done. It was obvious he wanted nothing to do with it and was very happy it was over and done. He had no idea what he had just done to us and really did not even seem to care. Nothing I said even mattered. The deal was done. The deal had been signed before I had ever gotten there and there was nothing I could do.

Afterwards I just sat on a bench in the courthouse and watched the people walk by. This was a different courthouse where the prosecutor resided, not the one where Martha worked, so I could sit out in public without being attacked. We lost, I thought to myself, there was no hope now. The state had thrown us to the wolves. My body felt beaten and I was worn out from running around trying to keep my children safe. It was as if I was in quicksand. The faster I ran the faster I sank. I had one kid in a mental institution miles away and three kids going to school, trying to hold down my job, and court cases every week. Let alone my crazy ex trying to wreak havoc at every turn. It was too much. Now I would have to go into the lion's den. I had been there before and found no justice there. I felt hopeless, like everything was against us.

Now I would have to go back to kangaroo court. Where I knew I could not win. After all the judge had nearly dried Martha's tears for her last time I was there. At least we learned the truth. She would have been imprisoned except the state would never put her there. The children would have to pay and pay for her to lose her parental rights.

They never questioned if Martha was guilty or not. They all knew she was but they did not want to be the ones to do anything about it. So this is the price you pay for speaking out about child abuse. To be treated like criminals and shoved under the rug like a piece of dirt that no one wanted to see. All the lawyers and everyone I asked said that in private court the person with the most money would win. Well, at $400 per hour, a working man's savings disappears fast when having to pay lawyers. I just hope I had enough money and I wish someone would just tell me who to pay to get out of this mess before I lost all my children.

Chapter 17

ANGEL OF MERCY

N ow that the criminal case was over, the private court summoned me again. This time I had no time to plan anything. Brant was being released from the hospital and I was to appear in court in about a month. Brant was being released and I was to have an exit interview with the director of the hospital to talk about Brant's treatment going forward.

I was very impressed with them: the doctors, staff, and guards had been very nice to us and they seemed very surprised that we visited Brant so much. They said this it very rare, although a compliment, it was very sad.

My father decided to come with me and we were both welcomed into the director's office. She was a stately woman, well dressed and attractive even though the worry around her eyes showed. No doubt from the pain she saw every day from the children on her floor.

She had talked to and seen Brant every day since his stay here and knew everything I needed to know about his medication and treatment. After we discussed this at length and I thought she was about to dismiss us, she stopped to mention one other thing for us to talk about. She said, in a matter-of-fact tone, "Ninety-nine percent of the children who come here have no one or their parents are on drugs and just enjoy beating or molesting them. They feel much safer with us than anyone they know out there which is very sad. So when I see a parent who loves their child and tries to do the right thing I go out of my way to help them."

She continued, "I have talked to Brant at length about what his mother had done to him and what he would like to see happen. He said he would like to see her imprisoned but since that is no longer an option, he would just like you to have full custody and no visitation with her."

The director continued by saying, "Listen closely to what I am *not* able to tell you." I was puzzled, but I think I was catching on. She said, "I am not able to let you know if I can show up and testify on Brant's behalf at the next custody and visitation hearing. I also cannot tell you that I used to work with those lawyers and judges in that very court and I know exactly how to word my testimony and tie their hands so as to give you full custody. I also cannot say that we have a wonderful counselor here at the hospital who would protect the best interests of the children if they were to see her. So what do you think?"

My father and I looked at each other and I turned to face her," Exactly what are you say…" she cut me off and looked directly at me.

She leaned forward as if to say a secret and motioned me to move closer, "I cannot tell you these things but if you were to ask me, I can."

With a nod I finally understood what she was trying to say between the lines. I asked her to testify for Brant at the custody and visitation hearing and immediately set up counseling at the clinic downstairs with the counselor she mentioned.

My father and I talked at length about this meeting. Evidently according to some government rules, the people who can help in these situations are not allowed to. Unless they are asked in a certain way. If you have no idea what you are doing then you cannot get help. Beyond stupid, yes, but we finally met someone who would give the children a voice and stop the court from running right over us.

Maybe we had a chance, after all, but I was not holding my breath just yet. Meanwhile, Brant could not handle returning to school, so I made a kind of deal with the school for him to do his homework at home. The teachers at the school liked Brant and they went out of their way to help us out. My parents had moved in with me because I could not be everywhere at once. Also it was not safe leaving the children home alone after the bunny incident. They also knew I had been pushed to the limit and came to keep me from doing something stupid, as my dad said.

The deal with the school after only two weeks was fading fast and they wanted him to return or truancy would become an issue. Someone, I thought, must have put pressure on them to not grant Brant any special favors. I am sure I knew who that was. After a few meetings with the principal and school officials, I quickly realized they were "all talk" with regards of helping us through this. They suddenly did a three hundred and sixty degree turn and gave me ultimatums as if everything I told them was a lie.

I talked to the children's counselor who said that patients with PTSD were often triggered by remaining in the place where the incident happened, which was of course was where we lived. She also said that Brant would never feel safe outside or inside the house and that a move to an entirely different area was the only answer to Brant getting better, and at this point was the only option. The stress of being in an area where his mother could show up at any time was too much for him to handle. Martha had completely broken him. The most outgoing person I had ever met, the light of our world, would not leave the house. I was out of moves and they had trapped us. All we could do was hope and pray. It was in God's hands now.

So since I was going to court anyway, I had my lawyer make a motion to let us move out of town but stay in the state which was the law. If this was not granted I had no idea what I was going to do because there was no way Brant would go to school. Just another impossible situation made worse by Martha's family influence in town. We really needed out. There was no place left to go in this town. Martha's family had all but run us out.

The following month was a whirlwind. My new lawyer wanted me to do a deal with Martha's attorney to the point of threatening that we might lose custody altogether. I could not believe it. Martha had been convicted of two of three counts of simple assault of which the grand jury wanted to make felony counts of child abuse. Yet here was Martha trying not for just visitation but for custody and there was a really good chance of her getting this. I knew exactly what would happen if she got custody. Just her getting visitation put Brant in the hospital and to a lockdown facility. How in the world does this make any sense? It did not, but it was happening anyway.

For some reason my lawyer had changed to Martha's side. It seemed that she was arguing with me for Martha's rights not vice versa. The other thing that really bothered me was that my lawyer was also a member of the state board for abused and neglected children. It was why I felt good about hiring her in the first place, but now I could see that she was not for child's rights whatsoever.

My lawyer also fought me on having the head of the psychiatric ward testify and would not subpoena her. I finally told my lawyer to subpoena her or I would just go to her house and pick her up myself. She, after all, was our only chance. So not trusting my lawyer to do so, I called the director to let her know about the court hearing date and time myself. The director said that she had not heard from my lawyer but had found out on her own about the court date and thanked me for calling. It is unbelievable. Here I am, going into one of the biggest court days of my life, and my lawyer was not working for me. It seemed the deck was stacked against us and, again, there was absolutely nothing I could do about it.

Chapter 18
COURT SURPRISE

The day had come and Martha's attorney and the judge had the proceedings moved up an hour. I could not reach the director of the psychiatric facility to inform her of the change in time. I was sure this was all planned ahead of time. To change it at the last minute so she would not be there to testify. Where was justice again? Is there no law and order? These were only a few of the questions going through my mind. How can this happen? We have done everything they asked but no matter what evidence we bring forward it did not matter and now they were even making last minute changes to court time so a witness would not be able to make it.

The courtroom was full. Martha brought her entire family with her which probably numbered about thirty or so and I had my parents and a couple of my brothers and their wives. Thank God I had them there as I was not so sure I would not be stoned to death right there in the courtroom. I remembered last time when they had to sneak me out the back door. I felt like a target in a carnival game. Just waiting to get hit.

The room was quiet and it was just my lawyer and me. Which meant I was all alone in front of the courtroom with no help from anyone anywhere. If the director did not show up, they would nail us to the wall. I could feel the clock ticking and still no sign. Had they even contacted her at all? I doubted it. With only a minute to go I thought it was over and then out the back door I saw her for an instant. She made it! Relief flooded over me but it was soon washed away by the hate Martha's family was throwing my way. From the looks they were giving me I did not think I would get out of there alive. I was wondering if this was a courtroom or a public execution.

I could feel their eyes on me but there was hope. The voice for the children was here and now it was not just the kids and me in this fight anymore, we had professional testimony. As I felt that wave of relief I could see the strain in my lawyer and Martha's lawyer as we all saw the director at the same time. Maybe the deal they had evidently hashed out in the back room might be falling apart. The appearance of the director had totally changed the mood in the courtroom. They did not like it and that made me feel good.

Then the hearing began and my witness was called up. The judge seemed a little disturbed by her presence. He seemed a little nervous and maybe even a little scared or was I just seeing things. She had definitely changed the vibe in the courtroom either as an unknown entity or a known one. It had changed the entire court-room because they were no longer focused on me. Now the focus was on her.

Now everyone would know what Brant had to say about it from his therapist who seemed to know exactly what she was doing. She sat in the witness chair like she had done it a million times. Like she owned it and her confidence even made Martha's crooked lawyer shrink behind his desk. Her stately figure made the courtroom seem more legitimate somehow. My lawyer got up and asked the director exactly what had she learned from Brant in therapy.

From her first words, it was all over. She said, "In the children's first counseling session, when Martha told Brant to look her in the eye, turned out to be exactly what she said every time before she hit him." The she paused as if she was in a movie. That brief moment of silence was when I knew the children had won. In that instant it was as if time stood still and then in slow motion the judge fell back into his chair, Martha's lawyers eyes popped out of his head and he dropped the pen he had been holding and Martha's family ceased talking...for once.

We had only seen most of Martha's family on holidays and a couple of them were members of Casa, a group that spoke up for abused children. The entire courtroom held its breath as she continued to tell the court exactly what had happened to Brant and his sisters and brother. That with all patients of PTSD being in the place it happened would set off unexpected triggers and that a move would greatly help the children move on with their counseling. That any visitation should end until which time the children's new counselors deem it fit to resume.

When she finished, the director was escorted out of the courtroom and we never saw her again. The judge was dumbfounded. Either he knew no history of the case or he was a good actor. Martha started her bawling fit like last time when the judge had consoled her. The judge shook his bony finger at her and said, "That will not help you this time. There is definitely more here than meets the eye. We will take the director's advice and leave visitation up to the counselors and the father will retain full custody. The family will be allowed to move as long as it is in state and a family mediator will be appointed."

Boy Martha's family was mad. Except the ones that worked with Casa they disappeared and never showed up again. I had to stay until the courtroom cleared out; supposedly they were concerned with my safety. The bailiffs went out to try to clear a path to the back door so as to sneak me out again. I found it beyond ironic that the one who had terrorized the children all the years and been convicted of it got to use the front door while I was snuck out the back like some kind of criminal.

As I waited in the courtroom with my lawyer, one of Martha's sisters started screaming at me and attempted jumping over the partition to get at me. Her sisters drug her off laughing. This was no joke because the sister-in-law that was trying to get at me was about six foot two and weighed about three hundred pounds. No bailiff came and she was not rebuked in any way. I had almost been assaulted right there in the courtroom and no one would have stopped it. I bet if I had I tried to protect myself, I am surely the one who would go to jail for it.

I could not believe my ears. We had won and we could finally get out of here. No more police escorts, no more of the children being persecuted at every turn. As it turned out they were scared of the director. She changed everything. Through Brant's sacrifice we had found an angel and she had saved us. There are no words that I could ever say to thank her enough for what she did for us. She was truly a light in a dark place.

We packed up in record time with just the clothes on our backs. Everyone kept looking over their shoulders expecting the police to show up and somehow stop us from leaving. The only thing left was to go to the new counselor and meet this new mediator they had been talking about. I did not even know what a mediator did and unfortunately he was appointed by the court and I knew nothing about him except that I had to pay him which seemed to be the norm.

Thank God maybe the court cases were going to slow down. I had cashed in my 401K and it was almost gone. I needed to find a new lawyer again after the last disaster so I fired my current lawyer and moved to the last name on the list. Thank God she took my case and finished the divorce proceedings after we moved. After that was done I had to fire her too because she also stopped working for me and allowed me to make a big mistake, which at the time I knew nothing about what to do except for what she told me. Martha's lawyer had drafted a settlement which in the fine print said that I would have to return to that same court for any custody or visitation problems that would arise. This sentenced the children to the age of eighteen in the one courtroom in the state that was entirely biased against them. I found out later that this was totally false and that the custody and visitation hearings should take place in the county where the children reside. That would prove to be a big mistake. I still cannot believe that every lawyer who worked for us screwed us in some way. I paid them $400 per hour and still they screwed us.

I knew for a fact that if the director had not been there it would have totally gone Martha's way. I had hoped I would never have to go back to that courtroom again. Unfortunately I knew better. Martha would never quit. According to the law she could take me to court up to three times a year until the youngest child turned eighteen. I found out later that any further court cases should have been wherever the children resided. Which I would find out did not work out for me later. Martha's family seemed to control most of what happened in that town as I had seen from the police, the hospital, and in the very courtroom itself.

Meanwhile, during all of this Brant had been asked to join the American team in the Down Under Games in Australia for cross country. Due to his age and time he finished in the state competitions, it had qualified him to be on their team. I had originally turned it down because it cost five thousand dollars to go but Brant needed something to pull him out of the depression he was in since his hospital stay.

He was nowhere near the old Brant that handled life with a smile and a joke. That visitation had really taken its toll on him and being admitted to the hospital had somehow stolen his confidence. So I needed to decide if I would rather pay for more counseling or send him to Australia to give him something else to think about. I decided on the latter. However, since I was out of money, I took out my first credit card and maxed it out.

Upon the news he was going, Brant started showing signs of life again and even starting getting in shape so I guess that I had done in one moment what could not be done in several months of counseling. He even did some fundraising and I still have some t-shirts to prove it. Since we moved before his trip, I had to drive him all the way back just to put him on a cracker jack plane to fly around the world. I had not seen him this excited since who knows when. I gave him a hug before he got on the plane and handed him a cell phone which I had to rob from Peter and had not told Paul as a last minute gift and told him to call me.

For the look on his face at that moment, I would have paid all the money in the world. His light had come back and the brightness was blinding. He called when he first got there and then I never heard from him again. I would find out later that after our one and only conversation he had gone swimming in the ocean and dropped the phone and that was the end of that.

He would return a week and a half later almost the same old Brant. He had a tan and the worry lines around his eyes had faded and his smile was back. He had finished in the top one hundred out of three thousand runners and was very proud of that. Brant told us all stories of his many adventures like going on safaris and swimming in the ocean but the one thing I would never forget was the look on his face. The light I had always seen. It was back and it was brighter than ever.

I always felt that he was destined for great things and it discouraged me to see his light fade and nearly extinguished by his mother. Now we would see what "Brant unleashed" could do now that his mother could no longer try to destroy him. His sacrifice had truly saved us all because had he never gone to that institution we would have never met the director and it was that moment that gained us our freedom. Even in his weakness he had saved us. That special light survived and now burned bright again. I could not wait to see what he would do now. He had always been the boy that had always believed if you could think it you could do it. I was just waiting to see what he would and what he could do next.

It was when we first moved that my father told Brant about the power of lighting candles on the side alter at church. That no matter what you wanted, you could light a candle and say a prayer and as long as the candle stayed lit your prayer would go on. Brant religiously lit candles after that every Sunday and every Sunday after church we would wait for him to light his candles and say his prayers. Most days he would pray quite a while. He was a good Catholic, especially for a teenager, and the candles grew to mean a lot to him. I asked him once why he would light the candles and he said, "So my mother can never get any visitation to see any of us and so that no other child should have to go through what I have." More grown up than most grown- ups and only seventeen. He had seen too much and been through too much for such a young age. Now his life would be different and we hoped and prayed it would stay that way.

Chapter 19

STARTING OVER AGAIN

I had no doubts that our new counselor would be the best since she was recommended by the director and I was right. She was everything the first counselor had not been. She was good with children and made it all about them which is what it was all about. After our first brush with counseling she had to go a long way to convince any of us it would help but it did in its own way. Unfortunately, we did go through that first horrific event and after something like that, the children were never going to open up to a counselor no matter how good she was. She was soft spoken and very kid friendly with different games to play to get the children to trust her more. That was good because after we moved to my parents' place, we continued counseling there with her for a year and a half. She was a good five hours from where we lived but we did not want to rock the boat and go back to court to change it. Why change a good thing and we were all tired of court. After all, it was a miracle we got out the first time.

Now as good as meeting the new counselor was, the mediator on the other hand was an entirely different matter. I knew it as soon as we walked in. It was the same dingy rotten moldy office just like the first counselor we saw. But nothing prepared me for the man I met. A small man as old as the building itself with a cane that held up a very shriveled body, no doubt due to a few too many cigarettes, with beady eyes behind horn rimmed glasses. It was not his body so much but his demeanor as soon as he spoke. He was used to doing things his way and there was no other. Exceptionally stern I could tell immediately that the children would not like him and he wanted to speak to each of them one on one to tell their story again. The children would tell me later it was more of an interrogation than a telling of the story and he had made them feel like field mice. I mean, come on! Give these kids a break already. How many times would they be questioned and harassed, especially now, when they are just trying to cope with all of it and put it behind them.

After he was done with the children it was my turn. I was definitely intimidated by him and his voice grated my ears. He lectured me on how he was here for the best interest of the children and that what I thought did not matter to him in the slightest nor did what Martha thought. In fact, if it was true, that was exactly why I was here but I knew I would have a fight and a half with him someday. But for now he seemed all right. We would see him a total of three times which was fine with me because truly the man gave me "the creeps" just like the first counselor had. I think if I were to meet the devil in human form he would look and act just like him or Martha. They were the same side of an evil coin. Nevertheless, after nearly a year of counseling I could not do it anymore. The children could not handle school and being gone two weekends a month for counseling and to tell the truth I was totally broke from gassing up the car to drive five hours and trying to keep my vehicle running, I just could not do it anymore. The courts totally broke us.

So I proposed it to the children's counselor to try to find therapists in our area and she wrote a letter to the mediator explaining the situation. We found two more locally and they seemed very good. The mediator agreed, much to my surprise, and we switched to a town much closer to us which was both good and bad. Good that we would be closer to home and bad because the children would literally have to start over again with their stories for new people but they needed the long drive to end as I did.

I fired my last lawyer when the divorce and abuse cases ended so I needed new ones. I was on my fourth one now so I was getting used to it. There happened to be a new lawyer office in town and so I decided to try them out. I met with them and immediately liked them. Not only could they not believe how badly the children had been treated but they actually listened. This was the first lawyer that had ever been like that. They actually listened and believed me which was to say exceptionally nice for a change.

About six months after the children had moved to the new counselors I started receiving threatening telephone calls from the mediator about Martha getting supervised visitation with the children. I told him it was up to the counselors to decide that. He said he had spoken to them and the children did not want to see Martha. The counselors told him that it was not in their best interests.

The mediator demanded, "I am telling you that you need to orchestrate these visits immediately or I will order a court hearing!"

I told him, "I will not go against the children's nor the counselors' wishes. The last time Martha saw them, Brant ended up in the hospital."

He retorted in his manner-of-fact tone of voice, "I am well aware of what happened but Martha has rights too and she wishes to see the children and I will advise the court that you are unwilling to cooperate."

Now he had made me mad! I had not heard from him at all for six months and he had not seen the children in over a year. Let alone the speech "how he was only here to do his best for the children" was still ringing in my ears. All he talked about was Martha. The children had just changed schools and counselors and now he wanted to throw in visitation. Not only that, but he wanted us to meet halfway between Martha and us so we would be back to driving again. I knew this day would come. I knew it since the day I met him. Martha was finally pulling his strings too.

I calmly replied, "So I guess I will see you in court." This had been his fourth telephone call in which he called me several derogatory names and hung up. I was *sooo* glad that I was paying for this, not like the kids needed clothes or anything.

So, I would go back to court again. I did not want any part of going back there into that courtroom again. Once a person escapes that type of situation you definitely do not want to go back. Just thinking about it made it hard for me to breathe. So my new lawyers figured out a way for me to attend the hearing via phone. I had never been so relieved to hear that. My lawyer would have to be present in the courtroom while I would listen in from my lawyer's office.

I did not want to see that beady-eyed old man, the mediator, again. It felt like he burrowed into my soul every time I saw him. Nor did I wish to see Martha or her little troll of a lawyer either. I did not want to see any of them. I had had enough. The children's new counselors decided to testify and talked to each of the children at length about how they felt about it and they would be their voice. The day fast approached and with each day came that queasy feeling of anxiety. I just wished it to be over. I warned my new lawyer that he would not be warmly received. I do not think he believed me but he would find out soon. I felt a little sorry for him because I realized he did not know what he was getting into and by now I kind of liked him.

Then the hearing day arrived and the hearing began. It started with the mediator totally defending Martha and telling the judge that she deserved visitation rights. He also told the judge what a strain it had taken on Martha not seeing her children all this time. This had happened all too often somehow these court hearings always ended up being about Martha and not the children.

My lawyer quickly retorted that the mediator had not even seen the children in a year and was not thinking of the children at all but solely Martha's opinions. I could feel his beady little eyes through the phone. Thank God I was not there.

Then the counselors were contacted via phone and expressed what the children wanted. The children wanted no visitation of any kind nor contact with Martha. The counselors did a marvelous job and just like the director, were the true unbiased voice of the children. The judge ruled in the children's favor and no visitation was allowed but Martha could send the children letters in which she could apologize for what she had done to them. She never had to say she was sorry or even admit that she was wrong about the abuse she inflicted upon them. In none of the hearings had she once admitted what she had done and Martha had said more than once that she did not believe she had ever done anything wrong. If she did send the letters it could open up visitation at a later date.

However thankfully for us she would never admit what she had done to them. Therefore would not apologize for something in her mind was not wrong. So the children would never receive any letters and therefore visitation ended. Not that every day I did not think we would receive these letters and have to start all over again in court.

Chapter 20

LIVING WITH GRANDMA
AND GRANDPA

My lawyer would later admit that he could not believe how badly he was treated by that court and that he was not inclined to go back. So we would follow the rules and not cause waves. We would let it lie and count ourselves lucky that we got out alive.

Meanwhile, the move had worked. We were all a lot more relaxed now that we were three hundred miles away from that craziness over there. It was unfortunate that the children had to pay the price, yet again, by moving their home and school and leaving all their friends. Where the move had done a three hundred and sixty degree change for Brant, the rest of the children were having a harder time with it. None of them missed Martha or her family but they did miss their friends that they had lived near their whole lives.

Not only that, but we would live with my parents for a time. They had a large house and I had nothing left. I sold everything and spent every dime and more to pay lawyers. My parents stood by me through the whole affair and having them around made me feel better. I needed a break from the stress that had been going on far too long. Getting the children enrolled in a new school was like a full time job. Martha had access to their grades but was not allowed to talk to their teachers. Martha would of course do everything possible to break as many rules as she could before I could sit down with the principal and explain the situation. After I explained what was going on and had a couple of heated exchanges with them and Martha on the phone, it finally settled down.

Brant and Grandpa, who had always gotten along, became good friends now and had many exchanges about politics, farming, and the weather. They generally thought along the same line about things but it was very amusing to listen to them go on and on. Dad loved to tell stories about the old days and Brant was willing to listen to them. It was so much better than before but it was hard to get used to. The quiet would surround us sometimes like a warm quilt after all those years of the screaming and yelling it was like paradise. Not only that, but who could resist my mom's home cooking.

Brant was unleashed now, able to have friends and go to parties. Before Martha drove all his friends away and never let him go anywhere. Brant took full advantage of it now and he became popular immediately because of course he was a likable guy. And he had that certain something you just could not resist. He had charisma and charm, a pure light that surrounded him at all times that other people seemed to feed off of, like some kind of energy drink. He excelled in school and started his new school halfway through his sophomore year. He joined the track team in the spring. He was an excellent runner but did not quite fit in to the relay team. That team had been together since birth so he was allowed to do his own thing. He would of course tell you he did not like running but did it because he was good at it. That was Brant for you always laughing it off. He loved the fact that no one knew what happened and we kept it a secret. The children felt they could be themselves except whenever people wanted to know about their mother. It was a forbidden subject.

The children decided that I should not call Martha, their mother, anymore they did not feel she deserved it and she became the past. Even though counseling made them try to remember, the children just wanted to forget like it was a bad dream. After all, everyone grows up with their own monster under their bed. Unfortunately for us, Martha was theirs and she was real. They hated counseling but they got used to it. They really just wanted it to end but I knew until they were eighteen they would have to go in case they needed someone to speak up for them in court.

Brant excelled in track and soon made quite a reputation in town. He would run the eight hundred, the sixteen hundred, and the thirty-two hundred meter run at every track meet. This was more like an iron man competition. What was even more amazing was that he placed in every event. It was fun to watch him run. It was like a fluid motion like a deer running in the field. He made it look easy even though you knew it was not.

In between you could see him socializing with his friends and by now he had a lot. He would always stop and talk to the younger kids down through grade school no matter how busy he was. That was why, I am sure, that he was almost late to some of his races. He talked to older people too and if you said hi he would stop and have a conversation. He did not care who it was or what he was doing, everyone was his friend.

He would even talk to other guys while they were running, which amazed me. I could not believe anyone could talk and run at the same time like that. I asked him once if that was not a whole lot more work than it was worth and he replied, "It gives me something to do between laps and I never really noticed it." I looked at him quizzically and he laughed, that was the way he was. Somehow he had turned horror into laughter and it really worked for him. I still remember the looks on the other runners face when Brant would start talking to them during the race. The runner would be blue in the face from trying to pass him and Brant would start talking. They looked dumbfounded that anyone could be talking to them and many of them lost stride from laughing. It was hilarious to watch.

Brant always wanted a farm since he was very little and the children wanted their own place to call home so with help from Grandpa, we bought a little place right down the road. It was a little ramshackle house that mice would not even live in but we patched it up and moved in. It was a beautiful place in a small valley with a long driveway that was so remote if someone did not show you the way you would never find it. It was a beat up little house with a falling down barn. There was a huge pond right behind and a beautiful shelter belt surrounding the buildings. It was a nice quiet place off the beaten path. It was what we needed when we needed it.

It was in bad shape but it was ours and the children loved it. It had an old trailer house on it for storage that no one had lived in for years. I should have burned it down but Brant quickly claimed it for himself and his friends. There was never a weekend it was empty for the rest of his high school career. He always had someone over to hang out in that old dust bin. I could not believe anyone would want to spend time in it since it smelled of mice and you had to be careful not to fall through the floor. But Brant always talked them into it. They had a lot of fun in that old crate and nearly burned it down several times trying to heat it up with a wood stove.

Brant was a junior now and surprised me by joining the football team. Now this was a little school of maybe two hundred students in high school and nearly all the boys were on the football team. Not only did they need all the boys just to have a team but the town was widely known for their football teams. So Brant did both cross country and football since they were at the same time. He was also in chorus and in the school plays. I really do not know where he found the time.

He practiced for cross country in the morning before school and football after school. Somehow he made it work and did well on both teams. There was never a time he was not high-fiving guys on the team and yelling encouragement at them in games. Although he did not get to play much on the football team, since he had only just started and was a little small for it, you could tell he was beginning to work that magic again. I saw his power was back, his charisma, his confidence, and positive influence like the eye of a hot flame. I could see the light in his eyes again. It had not taken him very long to come back. It amazed me the way he had gone from being scared to leave the house to going to a new school. Not only making lots of friends but excelling in his studies and his sports. There seemed to be no stopping him now.

The children were still going to counseling and getting really tired of it, but it was necessary. Even though the road had been long and tiresome my mother pointed something out to me. The children had school pictures and my mom always replaced the old ones with the new. The former year, the kid's pictures looked like prison photos. You could see the stress in their eyes, the worry lines, much too old to be of children. The new pictures had real smiles and their faces lit up. She told me things must be going all right, just by looking at their faces.

She was right. Things were finally going our way. The court hearings came and went and the children excelled in school. It was hard to adjust but they were doing well. Brant found his own world now and was always on the go; to sporting events or friends' houses. I let him go, after all he had a lifetime to catch up on and he did his best to miss nothing. As far as I know he never slept for those two years of high school he just had too much to do.

The sports award banquet was at hand and since the children's old school had nothing like it I did not know what to expect. I was busy working trying to make enough for us to live on our own. Brant told me that I did not need to come because he was not up for any awards. After all, he had only been in his new school for not even a full year yet. So I ended up working and just letting him go. Brant returned late that night after the other children had gone to bed and I had just arrived home from work. I asked him how it went.

Brant said nonchalantly, "Ooo not so good I just won this," he handed me a trophy.

I was astonished and said, "I thought you said you weren't supposed to win something tonight."

He smiled and said, "I did not know about it."

I looked down and read it and it said, «Most Inspirational" for track. It was like someone had knocked the wind out of me. The boy, who not even a year ago, had been in a mental institution, locked down because he might be suicidal, had won an inspirational award. I said gasping a little for air, "Good job man! "I gave him a bear hug, maybe even a little harder than I thought. My chest felt like it would burst maybe I was having a heart attack.

Brant yelled, "Easy! It's just an inspiration award."

"Yeah right," I said a little sarcastically and as I let go and turned away before he could see the tear come to my eye, "it's a big deal to me!"

Brant laughed and said, "Just wait till next year then," and with a wink he disappeared to bed. What a day, what a day! I would not miss any of these days anymore! This was a turning point for him and for me. We were finally going the right way.

School came and went and Brant's junior year was done. He had not only made friends of everyone in the school but everyone in town. He also made a best friend. Something he had never had. A guy, Brady, in his class and a giant compared to Brant. They made an odd couple but they were the best of friends. Kids came and went all summer and it was the best summer I could remember. We had never known such laughter and excitement. We had finally gotten used to counseling and there was always a court date looming but the further away we got in time the better things got. We went boating and had cookouts in our yard. Everything we should have always been doing, just the way a real family should.

Chapter 21

SENIOR YEAR

The new school season was starting and I asked Brant just how he thought the football team would do. The year before was the year they were supposed to go all the way and they fell flat on their faces in the playoffs. This year they lost most of their starters and there was a lot of talk around town that it would not be much of a year. Brant's class were seniors and it was a small class so there were only about six seniors going out.

Brant looked at me and said," We are going to win the championship."

I looked at him and said, "Aren't you setting your sights a little high? After all, last year didn't turn out too good." I did not want him to get his hopes up.

He turned and looked directly at me and said, "All I have to do is tell them they will win and they will win." giving me his usual smile and wink walked away off to school.

Normally I would have thought nothing of it, but I did see this boy lead a baseball team to a championship that they had no chance of winning. So why not? One time could be a freak accident but two times? Then there would have to be something more to it than that.

Brant was running cross country and playing football again. His times in cross country were his best ever and he was coming

113

so close to breaking the school record and leading the pack. He always got faster as the year progressed but something happened half way through the season and he just plateaued and stayed the same. You could tell he was giving his all but something seemed to be holding him back. What started as a banner year ended with him in the state competitions finishing in the top fifty. I just could not shake the feeling something was wrong but he had still done great anyway. Of course Brant would not go to the doctor and told me it was all in my head.

Now football, on the other hand, had become Brant's favorite sport. Although he did not get to play much, he was always encouraging everyone and slapping players on the back and keeping them fired up. The times he did play he would go all out and got a lot of tackles for as little as he played. You could tell when Brant started shouting everything changed. The team actually did do much better when he cheered them on. Brady, Brant's best friend, literally ran over the other teams and Brant seemed to know just how to fire him up. They had remained unbeaten half way through the season and were about to face the toughest team in the conference. They had been championship contenders for the last three years and this year was no different.

They were ranked second and we were third, flip-flopping in the rankings most of the year. The game got off to a bad start and we seemed to be beaten as soon as we got there. By half time we were trailing by two touch downs and they were running right over us. When out in the distance you could see lightening and hear the thunder. There had been no reports of bad weather in the area and yet there it was. It hit the field in a blind fury of driving rain and lightning so bad that the game was postponed to the next day. We did not drive even five miles towards home when we drove out of it and there was nothing. It was as if it was only over that football field and nowhere else. This storm had never been reported because it was not supposed to be there. It appeared a mile out of town hit the game and totally disappeared like it never happened.

When we showed up the next day no one wanted to see the end of that game it looked really bad for the home team. But as soon as the ball was kicked off it was a totally different game. The Wildcats would never score again and we made five touch downs in one half of the football game to win. It was an extraordinary ending to game that everyone was convinced we would lose. It got me thinking exactly how powerful were those candles that Brant lit because this seemed to be way more than a coincidence. It sure seemed like Divine intervention saved our team from defeat that day as Brant's light shone.

The team would go on undefeated 11-0 to the championship game. Now Brant had done his part and even gave an inspirational speech at a pep rally that had everyone talking for weeks. It not only was inspirational but funny as well. The kids loved it. But the team we faced for the championship was tough. They had, just this year, been lowered to nine man football and had been winning championships in eleven man. We did not match up to them at all. They were big and they were fast and had multiple players they could switch out because their school was twice as big as ours.

Brant of course was optimistic through it all but it was a David and Goliath game and we were David. For those of you who do not know who David is, he was a boy in the bible who faced a giant and killed him with a sling shot. The game was in a huge indoor arena nothing like we had played in before. You could feel the electricity in the air as the teams descended onto the field and I could see Brant slapping guys on the back and getting them fired up for the game.

We made the first touchdown and drew first blood but the rest of the half was theirs. They would make three touch downs and we would trail 22-8 at half time. It looked like it was over but I had learned a long time ago never to underestimate Brant and his power of prayer.

Our team would come back from the half fired up. Our defense would shut them out for the rest of the game. We would score two touch downs in this half; one of them in the last two minutes of the game. We would score and win the game 24-22 what an unbelievable comeback. It had been that one-in-a-million game where the underdog would come back and win.

It was surreal to go down on the field. The players were on cloud nine and when I found Brant he gave me his wink and said, "I told you so."

I grabbed him and hoisted him into the air and yelled, "You sure did kid, you sure did!" For us life had been hard but that day we were winners for the first time and it felt good. I never doubted Brant again. I knew that if he wanted something bad enough there was nothing he could not do. Like I said, once was maybe a fluke, but twice was something else. His candle-lighting worked. The light that shone on that field after the game was so bright, so Divine, that is something we would never forget. After all our strife, all our grief, to end up here at this point was more than anyone's heart could take. I knew that my son and his candles had done this. He had brought us out of the darkness and into the light. A light so bright that even the biggest darkest shadows hid from its glory.

Brant would turn eighteen during that football season and you could see a weight just lifting off of him. He quit counseling, on his own accord, because he could make his own decisions now, as an adult. He told me as we celebrated his birthday that the most special thing about it was that Martha could no longer hurt him. He had beaten her. I felt relieved to see him this happy. The greatest thing he had to celebrate was that his mother could no longer hurt him. He should have never had to feel like that in the first place, but it was a relief to know she could not get to him anymore.

Brant did not play basketball. He called it his down months between the rest of the sports. He somehow became the MC however for the basketball games and did not tell me about it. I found this out from his sister. So my parents and I made it to the last game to hear him announce the teams. He had been nearly speechless at home during basketball season because he lost his voice so many times. I soon found out why.

He not only announced the players, but had his own rendition of the pre-boxing fight tagline, "let's get ready to rumble." I was totally stunned when I heard him as the announcer. His voice was not only big, it was huge!How such a voice could come from him I could not tell you. It was just like hearing a professional in Las Vegas or something. It sure was something to hear. I asked him how he made his voice sound like that and he said, "I just opened my mouth and it came out." And again, with his usual smile and wink he ran off with his friends laughing. I began to think there was nothing he could not do.

He would wind up with track season at the end of his senior year. He started out strong and in the first track meet ran his eight hundred meter run in two minutes six seconds. He always gained ten seconds every year since he started so it looked like he was about to break the school record. But he would not be able to even match that speed in the next few track meets. Seeing that something was wrong again, I took him to the doctor.

Before we could get in to the doctor, the regional competition was already right around the corner. The doctors took several tests and found out that Brant's body could no longer break down potassium properly and that he would be all right if he quit running. The running was more than his body could take. Well, to say the least I was mad. Brant had put so much work into it. He should not have had this happen to him now. This was HIS year. He had a full ride scholarship for cross country and track already in the works and now it was gone. I had been venting to Brant all the way home about how unfair it was to him when suddenly he said, "Dad, I don't need to run anymore." I kept ranting on, I had not even heard him. Then suddenly he yelled, "Stop, Dad. I don't need to run anymore."

Then I replied, "What do you mean…" then it dawned on me he did not need to run anymore. He had been running from Martha all his life and that was how he coped with it, he ran. Now he did not need to run any more. I said a little bewildered, "You don't need to run anymore."

Then he smiled at me and I smiled at him. "You don't need to run anymore!" I slapped him on the leg and said, "Well how about some ice cream then?" I never brought it up again and Dairy Queen ice cream always brought everything into perspective. On the way home Brant fell asleep just like he always did after ice cream. I looked over at him. There was my boy all grown up with legs like an Olympian on his skinny little body. He had been through so much but he had finally beaten Martha. No more would he have to run from her. He would control his own destiny now on.

Brant would finish out the year in track and he and his friends would have a great time. He would not qualify for the state competitions for the first year ever, but that was fine. He did not need to run anymore. He had won the most inspirational award on every team he had been on for those two years in high school. Further testament to that special light he carried with him always.

Brant had never actually had a birthday party with friends. Martha had never allowed it. He had gone to a few but never had his own. So for graduation I thought it was about time he had a big party. After all he had been through, I decided we needed to celebrate. I had nearly lost him two years ago and now that he turned eighteen and it seemed the dark cloud that followed him everywhere was lifted for him at least and that needed to be celebrated.

So I began to plan a huge party at the farm. I sent out over one hundred and fifty invitations, ordered balloons and enough food to feed an army. The children and I made a huge pile of trees in the middle of the yard for a huge bonfire. It was going to be epic.

I had decided since each graduate was reserved two seats at graduation that I would bring Grandma up front with me. Since she had been such a big part of his life growing up. She was ecstatic. I had never seen her so excited or nervous in my life.

The graduation ceremony was short and when it came time for him to give his rose to his mother he gave it to Grandma and her eyes filled with tears. I of course gave him a bear hug and squished the stuffing out of him, shook his hand and said, "You made it bud! I love you."

At which point he gave me his usual smile and pushed me away and said, "Sure, sure whatever. Don't embarrass yourself," and with a wink took off. Then they walked across stage and I could not believe it. Brant made it. After all the things that happened he made it. No one even knew everything he had been through to get to this point. I had never seen him so happy and it was one of the most monumental days of my life.

Out of the one hundred and fifty invitations I think nearly eighty percent showed up; family and friends young and old. Just when I thought I might have a few leftovers the entire football team showed up. Our little house was more like an assembly line as people filled plates and went outside since there was nowhere left to sit in our little house. It was unbelievable how many people came and how much they ate. I ordered several roasters full of barbecue meat and when the football team was done there was hardly a sandwich left. Everyone was laughing and having fun.

We had a large flat field next to the house so the kids found some golf clubs and a bucket of balls and had a driving range contest which was quite comical. But not nearly as funny as when all the high school kids went down to the lake and with a small child's riding toy they had found in the barn. They made a runway to the lake with a ramp at the bottom. Those huge football players would take turns sitting on that little car and would ride it into the lake off of the ramp. They picked up enough speed so that even the largest of them got some air time before the giant splash as they hit the water. Then afterwards they lit the bonfire and sat around drying out.

People stayed so long that I had to find some hot dogs and marshmallows for the fireside. It was what Brant had always wanted and only he could draw such a large crowd. People would be mad for years later that they had not been invited. I simply said I ran out of invitations. They would talk about that party for years and every once in a while someone still brings it up. Brant had finally gotten his big party and what a party it was.

Chapter 22

COLLEGE BEGINS

The summer went by in a whirlwind and I did not see much of Brant. He spent a lot of time with his friends and working that summer. He was excited about college and had it all planned out. He had received lots of scholarships through his hard work and diligence. He had decided to join a special group at the college they called the honor society. Many colleges had these and having never gone to college myself this was all news to me.

When we moved here, somehow the transcripts from where we had come from never arrived. I am sure this is thanks to Martha's families influence at the school. This severely handicapped Brant's and the other children's GPA. So when Brant applied to the honor society he got turned down because his grades, although good were not quite good enough. But once Brant put his mind to something, nothing stood in his way. So he applied again with a long letter telling the school exactly why they should let him into this rather prestigious club. Of course the next thing you know, he received a letter stating he had been admitted. I am not sure how or why he got accepted but it was Brant and he was still lighting candles so I never questioned it.

Then I learned what the honor society was all about. They had their own dorm rooms set aside from the rest of the students. Oh

121

great, I thought, he had just joined the snob club, but I was still proud of him. The more I learned about them though, the more I liked the idea. We needed to go to a meeting together about the honors program and just what to expect from it. Brant told me that I did not need to go if I did not want to but I wanted to see for myself just what he had gotten into. So I went along but Brant had a cheesy grin on his face the whole way and made me wonder what was in store. I asked him several times what was on his mind but he would only shrug and smile. During a two-hour drive this was quite annoying but I knew something about this was very funny to him.

We finally arrived and when we got to the room I understood why Brant had been smiling the whole time. I was totally out of place. I was a farm boy from the sticks and these were rich people. I was surrounded by polo shirts and designer shorts. It looked like a meeting for a country club. I was dressed in my farm cap and blue jeans and my best plaid shirt. They looked at me like I was going to rob them or something. I looked at Brant and his giant smile turned into a laugh. He knew about it the whole time and that was why he was smirking the whole way here. Well, let him get his laugh I was not sure if he had just bitten off more than he could chew anyway.

No one would sit at our table. I was sure that I frightened them. The last two groups that entered were the unlucky ones and ended up our table. After they found out I did not bite it became quite enjoyable. I also found out every student in this club was either a wannabe lawyer, doctor, or businessman. Brant decided to be exactly what he had wanted to be since he was a child. He wanted to be Indiana Jones. So he was a history major with an archeology minor.

He even got the Indiana Jones hat made of alligator skin while he was in Australia, which when he proudly wore it, he definitely looked the part. It seemed to me that after the day was done, that I could not run into any more parents whose child was going to be a teacher. So Brant had gone above and beyond again. Of course by the end of the day Brant made several new friends and I knew he was going to excel. I had always had the feeling that he would do great things and I hoped I would live long enough to see it.

He had of course picked a school that took history and archeology serious. The history class would take a field trip his junior year to be the crew on a boat and sail around the horn of Greece looking at ruins all along the way. The archeology class would spend their summers digging in ruins in Venezuela looking for lost treasure. I could not wait to hear the stories he would have to tell when he went on these adventures. It was right up his alley.

He did of course still have certain health issues, thanks to the trauma Martha imposed on him. PTSD never goes away or fades with time, it is a constant battle which can attack at any time. Small things set off triggers and there is nothing you or anyone can do about it. Brant was good at coping with it and to meet him you would never know anything was wrong.

He was always all smiles and joking around and made everyone feel better about themselves. The reason why he could influence people to do such miraculous things like in football and baseball was that he thought so highly of you that you did not want to disappoint him. He would, in his way, gently push you to be more than you thought you were. It was a gift he had, a way about him that you did not notice. You needed to see how it affected you, not only in the moment, but in the time you knew him. You would never have known that for all his laughter and jokes, he would have to fight every day just to be normal or what everyone thinks is normal.

He had a lot of trouble sleeping, he did not eat right, and sometimes his memories, what he could remember, were confused. He had trouble taking tests because he had no memory recollection. It had been stolen from him by the trauma he had endured. So he and I would go through many memory games until we found some that helped him get through it. He also did not like to take pharmaceutical drugs so we found organic pills that helped him naturally fall asleep. It was a struggle for him and yet he could make you feel so much better about yourself in only a few minutes. It seemed like his mission in life to make his family and friends happy.

It was on one of these such days I had this conversation with Brant. His memories were not always there but when they were, they were sometimes all jumbled up and confused. I was the only one who could help him sort them out and this happened on our way home from college one day. He wanted to know why I did not stop Martha sooner and how come I, like she said, knew all about it and I did nothing.

At that moment, I pulled the car over, stopped and looked him directly in the eye. I said, "She lied to us both Brant I tried to get away from her sooner but it did not work. You saw how it was. We barely escaped when you were older. When you were young we would have had no chance. When you were young I tried to keep her away from you so she could not hurt you but I could not be everywhere at once. If there could have been any way I could have kept it from happening I would have. I did not know how cruel she had been to you when I was gone. I would have picked you every time. I am sorry I should have never married her and if I would have known I would have picked better. I should have given you a wonderful mother I am sorry."

There were tears in both our eyes now and I gave him a hug. Brant said while wiping off his face, "I guess she fooled us both."

"Ya but it's over now so remember if you ever need anything just call and I will be there bud." He smiled at me and I smiled at him we both knew of the ice cream shop on the way home. From that day on we got past her, Martha, her lies had hurt us but from now on she would never control our relationship again.

That day my son and I became friends just like we had been when he was a small boy and his mother had not twisted what we had. It took me back to chasing that fuzzy blonde haired little boy around and around the living room with him laughing his head off. Now here he was a full grown man despite all the crap the world had thrown at him. He made it into the honor society and he had changed so many lives in such a short time. Yes, indeed he would do something great. I knew it now more than ever.

I decided since Brant would be leaving us for college that we needed a family vacation. We had never really had one. So since I did not have much money we decided to go see my uncle in Minneapolis. He lived alone since his wife died and said he would love to have us. It was about a six hour drive so I decided to let Brant be the navigator. We had taken the back roads so we could see more country. It was a beautiful drive. We went through so many little Norman Rockwell towns that I lost count.

Then suddenly after getting directions from Brant it appeared we were going in circles because I remembered seeing the town we were in before. I looked over at Brant and noticed he had the map upside down and had not noticed. We all had a big laugh at that. Mr. College holding his map upside down. We would never let him live that down!

When we finally arrived we packed as many things into the week as possible. We did it all, everything from the Mall of America to Valley Fair. We had a great time. I could not remember ever laughing so much. It was about time that we could finally enjoy life. As we returned home totally exhausted I remembered thinking what a great send off for Brant it was. It would be hard to see him go. But he had a mission to accomplish and I could not wait to see what it was. The potential for his future was endless and I knew he would succeed no matter what direction he went.

Move-in day on the campus was in a word, chaos. Parents and students and stuff, so much stuff. Tons of stuff going into dorm rooms too small for humans. I myself felt claustrophobic just standing in his room but Brant was loving it immediately. I had never seen so many kids so helpful and so courteous. It was a welcome change from teenagers that always hid from you. These kids seemed to grow up immediately upon entering the dorms. If it was an act, they were very good at it.

I would visit Brant as often as I could making sure he was remembering to eat and at least take a nap once in a while. He wanted us to come up for Halloween so Lily and I did. It was a big deal since it was Lily's birthday. My Halloween baby. Brant said the entire floor would be giving out candy. So Lily and I got buzzed in through the security door. We started early because we wanted to get back to town before dark for our annual trick-or-treating. We were totally surprised when we opened the door. We were nearly run down by a bunch of students wildly playing tag. We were almost run over several times before we got to Brant's room at which time the door opened and we were pulled inside and the lights went out. "Be careful," several voices said, "we are being hunted."

Now after a half hour of waiting in the dark it was time we were going. So I said, "All right it's time to go is one of you Brant."

The lights flicked on and we were surrounded by ghouls. Then with a rush they yelled, "Attack!" and they opened the door and ran out all except one. As he flipped up his mask, it was Brant, he said, "So what's up?"

I said, "What do you mean? We almost got run over three times and then we got hauled into a dark closet with a bunch of ghouls." We all burst out laughing. We talked for quite a while and I asked Brant, "Does this go on all the time?"

His smile stretched from ear to ear as he said, "Yeah." He filled Lilly's bag with candy and finally let us out with a stern order to run for it. I was not sure but I think he was using us as a human shield. So run for it we did. Lily and I laughed all the way home. She thought she could definitely get used to college life.

I stopped by again later that month because Ann had an instrumental contest in town so I stopped by to see Brant and bring him along to hear his sister play. I called Brant and he met me in the parking lot. He had just gotten in the car and we were driving away when he offered me an Oreo cookie. Now had we not been in a hurry I might have thought to myself, since when does Brant give away food especially cookies, but we were in a hurry and I took it and took a big bite. Have you ever have that feeling when you take a bite of food and there is just something not quite right about it? This was the exact feeling I had. The filling was minty, not the normal white creamy middle, and that was not right. I looked at him oddly, and he immediately started laughing.

My mouth was full of this weird cookie and something else that was making me immediately feel sick. Brant said, "Does it taste a little bit like toothpaste? Ha ha ha" He was laughing his brains out when I rolled down the window and spit it out. It was a prank of course.

It was also a dumb idea to spit it out the window, but I needed to get it out of my mouth! The wind was blowing the wrong way and everything I had spit out ended up right back inside the car on my shirt. Now I do not need to tell you what a chewed up Oreo slash toothpaste looked like on my shirt. Brant was almost on the floor as I wiped my shirt off with a napkin but you could have heard a pin drop when I said, "This may be funny now but paybacks are always worse because now you do not know when or where but I will get you back." Brant stayed silent evidently he had not thought of that but a few minutes later we were both laughing again.

We went to Ann's recital and then we spent the rest of the day in the dorms playing pool in the play room on the bottom floor. We played all afternoon and talked about everything. As the evening sun slowly sunk below the windows I decided I had better get going because it was a long ride home. I lingered a little longer, one more game because this is what I had been waiting for. Spending time with my kid, Martha a distant memory, just enjoying time together and hanging out. It had taken a long time, too long and now we needed to make up for it. On the way home I realized that this is what we had been waiting for. Just to feel normal for once and it was great.

Once school was out again and Ann had graduated, we had another party. It was not quite as big or as wild as Brant's but there were a lot of people. After Brant's big party however, nothing can ever match up to that, but we all still had a lot of fun. Brant decided to stay at school and get a job. I told him he could come home but he wanted his own space and to live on his own. He had gotten a job at Hy-Vee supermarket stocking shelves and he seemed to like it although it did not pay well.

Ann would be joining Brant at the same college next year. It seemed that the two that always butted heads missed each other. Counseling had all but ended. The counselors said they had gone as far as could and that if there were any problems to give them a call. When Brant quit I knew it would only be a matter of time until they all quit. It had been long enough.

Every counselor the children ever had ever seen told me they had never seen children that had no bond with their mother. That maternal bond with their mother never formed. It was as if she never existed at all to them. It made them very hard to treat since this was very rare. Even children who were sexually molested still wanted contact with their parent but mine never did. To me this showed how bad the abuse had been and now Martha was just a distant nightmare for them that did not exist anymore.

Brant always said he would leave on some adventure and not come back. He had talked of wild destinations and living in the jungle or some island in the sea. But now after a year on his own he had decided he would come back and live and teach around home. To me this was great news after all, I bought this place for them to have a home to come to and there was plenty of space for everyone.

I had been talking about doing more work on the house and one big project was to take a large old aerial antenna off the roof. The thing was all of twenty feet high and tied down with some heavy wire and it would take all of us to get it off. I was planting corn on top of the hill and it was my favorite spot because you could look at our little valley with the lake behind the little run down house and the barn with the hole in the roof. It was picturesque to see our little place while planting our next crop.

Then suddenly I see a little red car come zooming over the hill it was Brant home for the weekend. Soon after I saw them, all the kids were out there trying to take that antenna down. The boys were on the roof and the girls on the ground and it was quite a comical sight, even though I was hoping no one would break their leg. They were laughing at each other and having a good time making fun of each other. From my vantage point they looked like dolls running around the house. It hit me then, there they were, my children laughing and working on their house. I had not told them to, only mentioned it. I am sure it was Brant's idea but they were working together on their house, their home.

I slowed the tractor down. I did not want to stop for fear they might see me watching. Before my eyes it dawned on me. We were a family, finally after all these years we were a family. We had a home and the only loud noise to be heard was laughter, no yelling, just laughter. I got a little choked up watching my children in the soft sunlight of evening and the beautiful scene below. How long we had waited for this? I realized in this moment we were happy for once and everything was going right. How long would it last? Only time would tell. But for now we were what we always wanted to be. We were a family with a home full of laughter and no yelling.

Brant had decided to bring some friends home and it was the end of July. We had decided to do our annual chicken cleaning for the year and Brant decided to bring some of the college city kids to the farm for the experience. Most of them were girls so I hoped they would not get sick. But of course somehow Brant talked them into thinking this would be some kind of fun adventure. Brant always had lots of girls that were friends it seemed, but nothing serious which kind of tormented him.

Anyway, to our surprise, some of them had done this before and joined right in. It went well until we started to chop off the heads and some of the girls thought they had seen enough and headed for the house. It was their mistake because Brant chased after them with a dead chicken with no head and they went screaming. It was all I could do not to fall on the ground laughing. I thought my mom and dad would bust a gut. I am sure most of them would think twice before going on one of Brant's wild adventures again.

Brant told me of the many practical jokes they played on each other. One of them had even frozen Brant's car keys in a block of ice while he was sleeping. It took the whole day to thaw them out. They knew how to have fun and I have never seen a more closely knit bunch of friends. It seemed impossible that they had not even known each other a year ago.

Chapter 23

THE PHONE CALL

Brant stopped in one more time a couple of weeks later before school was to start. To pick on his sister and to pay me off for some money he borrowed. This surprised me because I had not put any pressure on him to pay me and did not expect it back. I worried over him living on his own with all the problems he had but he had lived the whole summer there without any help. I guess he was all grown up and he would be starting his sophomore year in college with his sister who would be a freshman.

I told him many times throughout the summer that he could come home anytime but he toughed it out. However he told me next year he would come home and work around here. I was glad to hear it because we missed his smiling face and jokes here at home. For some reason, when he was gone, it kind of left a hole. I knew next year the adventures would begin and we would see less of him and hoped he would come home before his year abroad.

It was a wonderful time we cooked out every night and the weather was cooperating which was strange. We just took time to be a family and played board games, did a little fishing and hung out. My children were growing up. Now Ann would join Brant in college and all the preparations were done for that. Bret and Lily were doing great in school and football and cross country were about to start.

We had not been in court for over a year. I had realized that and had counted it as a huge milestone. I had hoped that Martha had run out of money. It seemed the less the children heard about it the better and better they did. Their worry lines around their eyes were nearly gone now. They would never actually disappear because the damage had been done. It would torture them the rest of their lives but it was now manageable. Which is the most we had ever been able to say.

Brant was leaving for school and after I seen him sneak over to the gas barrel to fill his car, which was his habit every time he came home. I was standing in the doorway to the house and asked, "What, are you stealing gas?"

He answered, "Nah, that was somebody else," he said jokingly as he walked away. I saw him smile and wave and I felt the urge to run over and give him a hug like I always did before he left. He was in a hurry so I just waved. There would be plenty of time for hugs. After all we had our entire lifetime now that he was coming home to live. Then I watched the little red car race over the hill with the thought of seeing him next week.

I had finished all the crop work in the next week and Brant had decided he needed to do some things so he stayed at college. We had finished getting Ann ready to move in and the kids were having one last hooray before school started. They were all at friends' houses and I found myself home alone. It was eerily quiet which is something I had a hard time getting comfortable with. It seemed there should always be some noise.

I was tired. It was always a race to get the crop work done before some bad weather arrived but everything had gone perfectly. Which was strange because something always broke down, but not this time everything had gone right, and why not? I thought, as I sat in the recliner on a very quiet Sunday. The sun was shining on me through the window and all I could hear was a lazy fly buzzing somewhere in the kitchen.

I remember thinking how everything had been going right. There were no court cases ahead, the children were doing great and the crop work was done. It was the best things had been for as long as I could remember. As I drifted off, I relaxed. Something it seemed I had not done in a long, long time. There was always some disaster looming in the distance but not now. There was just the sun shining through the window on my face. It felt good to just relax and listen to that fly buzzing and the world was melting away…and then I heard it.

I was already groggy with sleep but I could hear it, the faint ringing of the telephone. I wanted to ignore it but it kept ringing and it was waking me up. Then I thought, what if it is one of the kids and they need something and I reached for it. Now had I known what answering that call would do to the kids, to me and everyone we knew I would have left it ringing. Even now I would have let it ring and it would still be ringing today because had I left it I would never have known and that would have been all right with me.

I did answer it though and still wish I had not. As the person on the other end of the line started talking I thought, maybe I was still dreaming that this was not real. It was a police officer and he said, "Is this Brant's father?" I shuttered completely sober now. What happened? Was he in jail? But no, something far worse.

The officer went on to say, "Your son was seen swimming on Backwater Beach. He was swimming with three friends. He did not make it across the river. He was last seen bobbing up and down going down river and has not been seen since. You need to get here." He calmly gave me directions as my still shaking hand tried to write them down.

My first thought was this is a joke, a prank, those college kids they were always having fun. Maybe one of them had stolen his driver's license and it was not him. Yeah, that's it. It could not be Brant. It could not happen to him. He had too many things to do. He was going to do something great, something big, I had always known he would. I could not go alone, I should not go alone. I called everyone, no one answered. Of course not, it was Sunday and everyone was boating or fishing. So I left alone to go find Brant and bring him home just like I had always done. I would bring him home.

One of my brothers, Fred, finally called me back and I told him what had happened. He was on his way back from vacation and would meet me in a small town along the way. The beach was a little over two and a half hours away. As soon as we met up I let him drive. I was in no shape with a million scenarios in my head and trying to think of all of them and none of them at the same time. The officer had said it had happened at approximately three o' clock in the afternoon. It was five o'clock now and it would be around seven thirty when we got there right before dark.

It was a long quiet ride. There was nothing to say just an urgency to get there and find out what happened. Maybe Brant got out and was lost somewhere or needed help. We had to get there because I needed to know.

We drove for what seemed forever. We followed the directions and this beach which was around ten miles from the college. All the kids hung out there. Brant talked about it more than once and told me often that I should go there with him some time. This was not how I imagined seeing it, not at all.

We finally got there and it had stormed the night before which meant the river's water level would be up and the water deeper than usual. The deputy was waiting for us when we got there. When we drove up I could see he was holding some clothing. Yep that was Brant's shirt, his sandals, and his wallet. I had seen them a hundred times. There was no doubt it was him. He had been swimming on a beach about two hundred yards from where we were by the boat dock.

Together, my brother Fred and I, walked to the water to see what we were dealing with. We had grown up by the river our whole lives and we had a lot of good memories of good times we had swimming, boating, and fishing in that river but this was not one of those good times.

We looked over the bank and together we caught our breathe. Never had we seen a more unforgiving part of the river than this. The water was high, high up into the small trees along the shore a good five feet above normal. The water was a swirling mass of bubbling water from the massive amount of rain the storm had produced.

We turned and looked at each other with our mouths agape. Why would anyone go swimming in that? I was never a good swimmer so I did not swim in the river and had taught my children to be careful around the river because it was very unforgiving. I had, however, gotten my children swimming lessons so I would not have to deal with this. Brant was a good swimmer, a very good swimmer in fact, and athletic. He should have made it out if anyone did. This water was bad even on a good day. Why would anyone swim it. The deputy said we needed to see the beach to understand. So in the fading light, Fred and I walked down a narrow path full of vegetation to see the beach.

We could not believe our eyes when we emerged from the thick trees and brush onto the whitest, largest river beach I had ever seen. You would have thought you were on a Caribbean vacation. Just white sand as you looked out over the river. It was exactly opposite of what we had seen not more than two hundred yards away hidden by trees and a bend in the river. It was shallow as far as you could see. A sea of sandbars with little pools no more than a foot deep. It was beautiful and breath taking no wonder the kids came here. This was the most beautiful beach on the river we had ever seen and we had seen a lot of it. But it was an illusion for as calm as this side was you could see what looked like a little rough water on the other side. What it turned out to be was three hundred feet of thirty foot deep water full of fallen trees from a caved in bank and this is where Brant had gone down.

From here on the beach it looked like paradise and there was no signs, no signals that there was a trap out there. It turned out that this was a type of challenge for a lot of college kids to try to swim it. The sheriff had just rescued two girls not more than a month ago, from the other side on a dead tree, who could not make it back after they swam it. So where were the warning signs? There were none. Leaving it up to the kids to make up their own minds about swimming it. This was stupid and I told the sheriff so. He simply stated that the government would be held responsible if there were signs. Since this was United States Army Corps of Engineer land, no signs were ever posted.

It did not matter, Brant had gone down in that fast water and when Fred and I saw it for the first time, we had looked at each other and knew. It was a miracle that any of those kids had made it out. That water was moving so fast and Brant was light he would have had to been Hercules to make it out. We walked along the edge of the river as far as we could get but it was impossible. The water was too high and the brush too thick there was nothing to do till the rescue boats got there which would be in the early morning tomorrow. The deputy told us he would stay till dark and that if we needed to, to go get something to drink or eat. Now would be the time.

So Fred and I went to a little convenience store just a few miles away and got some food and something to drink. I needed something stronger than pop to settle down because this looked to be a long night. I needed something to keep all the thoughts in my head from swirling around. So we grabbed some off-brand wine coolers which was all they had.

When we returned, the river had turned red with the setting sun and clouds rolling in again. It was an eerie feeling in the dark by the water. We shone our headlights over the black water and took turns yelling out so if Brant was out there he could hear and see us. The night was black, the clouds had come in, and it was so dark it looked like the darkness was eating the light from the headlights. There was not a star in the sky and it was like a tomb. It was quiet except for the sound of the river which used to relax me but now it just made me sick. Brant could be out there wounded or hanging on to a tree and all we could do was wait. Wait for morning on a night that never seemed to end.

This could not be the end for Brant. I always knew he was meant for something special. How could this be it? I could not believe, I would not believe it. After all we had been through to get this far just to have it end like this, was a nightmare. No way was this happening. Someone needed to pinch me and wake me up because this was not real. I prayed and I prayed like I have never prayed before. Please do not let this happen, please. Please do not let him be dead. I do not want to tell his brother and sisters this after everything was going so well. This was not it. I would not accept it.

Then Fred and I started talking about it. Fred said, "I bet Brant is going to jump out of the bushes laughing at how big a joke this had been."

I chimed in, "Yeah, that would be just like him." We laughed and then dead silence. I knew Fred was thinking what I was but I was glad Fred was here. It kept me from jumping into the water looking for Brant. I had spent my life worrying about him. I had always been able to fix whatever happened and bring him home. I was defenseless now, there was nothing to do but wait and it was killing me. This was Brant, he could do anything he would be all right I told myself. But I had seen the water that dark swirling water and I could not get it out of my head.

The humidity was stifling, I could not breathe, and then the mosquitoes came. They came by the thousands and forced us into the vehicle. You could see the thousands of insects in the headlights zooming into the darkness. I hated mosquitoes ever since I was a little kid and I hated them even more tonight. They were pests and if Brant was wounded they would be biting him relentlessly and he would not be able to do anything about it.

We had wanted to scout the other side of the river where Brant had gone down but we were told by the officer that there were no roads on the other side for about five miles. Now if he had gotten out he would have to walk five miles through that thick brush without shoes and only wearing swimming trunks. That would be tough but Brant was tough. He would make it. Maybe in the morning we would get word that they found him wandering somewhere. That would be great and I would not even be mad. I just needed to find him, that's all.

The night dragged on we drank the wine coolers but they did not help at all. They tasted horrible like someone did not quite know how to make cool aid and threw a bunch of nasty stuff in a bottle and called it a drink. I was glad Fred was there. My four brothers had always been there when I needed them just like my parents. That was what family was about, they stuck by you especially when things went bad. I had seen enough bad and I did not want to endure this alone.

Fred had been coming home from a vacation with his wife and kids and was exactly four miles away from this very spot on the interstate, at about the exact time Brant would have gotten into the water. Had I only known I could have called Fred and told him to tell Brant to not do it, just get out and go home. How could have we have known? It just seemed pointless to think about these things. It was a long, long night.

Chapter 24

THE WAIT

I heard about drowning victims before but I had never knew any. I realized by the next day that is a wonderful thing to not know someone who went missing in the river. There was nothing to do but wait. There was no one to yell at only volunteers helping. Different government agencies showed up at the first hint of light in the sky. They showed up with boats and tons of volunteers who had done this kind of thing before each vowing they would find him. The reality was that this could take days possibly weeks and maybe never find him if he had gone under. They said the first twenty-four hours were critical for finding him alive and we had already lost eighteen before they got all the equipment and personal there to look for Brant.

The rest of my family showed up. The kids stayed in school and my mom stayed behind to keep an eye on them. They knew what happened and they would be the first call when we found something out. My brothers and father were there and some of their wives too. I needed the support just to keep track of what was going on. There were constant boats zooming up and down the river they had cameras and were trying to look at the bottom of the river looking for a body. There were others driving along the shoreline looking for footprints where he might of climbed out of the river.

The place Brant worked, Hy-Vee, had donated food to the rescuers and I thanked them profusely. The manager even delivered it and told me how great a worker Brant was and that they all liked working with him. That Brant, he was always impressing people, it was just like him to make a great impression. And he had only worked there for the summer.

Then there was the press. The newspapers which had to be silenced because I did not want Brant's name released and have my crazy ex and her family show up. Things were hard enough without that and besides Brant would not want them here in a million years. He hated Martha and she did not deserve to be here causing trouble. Why should I have to think about that with everything going on I told myself? I should not have to think about it but I knew if she knew she would come and cause us all more grief.

By the second day I knew everyone's names and I was strung out. The stress of waiting was taking its toll and I had stayed up all night waiting again with the head lights on. By this time, I had received the speech that he may be dead and I should be ready for it. I would not listen. Until they found him and showed me his body, he was still alive to me. I would not let my mind go there.

Then as I was standing watching the boats go up and down and up and down the river. A bunch of volunteers walked past carrying snag hooks. Lots of them on long heavy line. Giant sharp snag hooks and I knew when I saw them what they were for. They should have warned me, they should have kindly said you might not want to see this and warned me. They did not and dragged them not ten feet in front of me.

When I saw the hooks I felt myself turn green. All I could picture was those big hooks sinking in Brant's body and I could not take it, I needed a break. So my brothers and I took a walk down the road. I needed not to see the river for a while. I could not watch them drag the bottom for Brant. But we did not get a few hundred feet down the road when we saw the news photographers and we turned abruptly so they could not get a clear shot of us. We did not need our picture getting out.

Those buzzards were no better than real buzzards pecking at my son's body. Trying to get a headline. They made me sick. So I would go back and watch them drag the bottom. There had been no word about anyone finding him or any lead to prove he was not in the river. I went home that night. The rescue teams said that it could be a long time until they found him, if at all. They river was constantly changing. Moving sand bars buried many things for years.

I had left home early and had gotten there at first light. The trip home had been a waste I could not sleep anyway. Now it was the third day and I was all right. I had thought if they did not find Brant there would always be a chance he might show up someday. That was fine with me. If he was not found, then there was still hope. It would be ok if they did not find him. Actually it would be great. My uncle Pete had shown up and it seemed to help. Then my cousin and my brother Sam's wife showed up. The more family the better it seemed. Of course they shielded me from the questions and the updates for I could not take it anymore. Three days was too long and now I did not even want them to find him. It just needed to be over. I could not stand on the dock watching the boats drag the bottom for my son anymore.

The sun had not shown since the day Brant had gone into the water. It was three o'clock and he had officially been gone for three days now. Then the sun came from behind the clouds and it looked as if the storm was over. I was looking at the sky when I felt a hand touch my arm. It was the sheriff with a very quiet stern look on his face. He said the words like he was ripping off a band aid, "We found him."

He went on to explain where he had been found about two miles down the river. I was not listening I had only heard his first sentence the rest was a haze. Him saying they had found him had made it real. My son was dead. Brant was gone. The boy who could

141

do anything and spread so much light was gone. It was more than I could handle. There was no words to be said hope had vanished into thin air.

What would I tell his brother and sisters? I had always been able to fix it. I had always brought him home after everything we had been through. I could not fix this. It was over as I had known as soon as I had seen the swirling water with Fred. I had failed, somehow I had failed. After all Brant had faced he had only the good part left and it was over just like that.

Now they were bringing in his body on a boat. I needed to see him one last time. I needed to give him a hug before they took him away. I walked toward the boat and all my brothers and my father stepped in front of me and in unison told me that I did not need to see Brant like this. They said I needed to walk away. There was no fight left in me.

I had fought so long for his life and now it was over. I wish now I would have held his hand and said goodbye. It would not have mattered what he looked like for I would see this moment in my nightmares for the rest of my life. I can only say that my imagination has to be worse than if I had seen the real thing. My younger brother, Ralph, would tell me later that it was not Brant anymore when they identified the body. He was not there anymore.

I turned and walked up the road. Where my heart had been was an emptiness like I had never known. Of everything that happened this is what I had dreaded the most. This had always been in my prayers, to please Dear God, never lose a child. I had told God many times to do what you want with me but spare my children. This was the one thing I knew I could not take. I wanted to see the last place he had been. I needed to see that beach it was the last thing Brant had seen and I must be there now.

So with my body that seemed to weigh twice what it normally did I trudged down the little path. There was a beautiful blue pool along the path. I had never seen it in the sunlight. It was like something mystical you would see on some remote island. Then I emerged from the brush onto that beautiful white beach. In the sunlight it was breathtaking in its beauty. The beautiful clear blue water with the stark white sand and the beautiful green trees and shrubbery. There was a giant old cottonwood tree log laying in the middle of the beach bleached by the sun. I walked over and sat on it looking at the water.

My uncle came up behind me and quietly asked, "We will be here if you need anything." He moved back toward the path. I knew why they were here they thought I might do something stupid like drown myself. The thought had crossed my mind for a fleeting moment and if I did not have any more children to think about I might have done it. I did not want to bear this pain it was too much, just too much. I would not leave my children to bear this pain alone they had lost enough.

I had not shed a tear and as I looked out across the river, I reached within myself for that strength that had always been there but it was gone. There was nothing left but a giant gaping hole that seemed to swallow all light. Then the tears came like a river that I could not stop and all the pent up stress of the last three days left my body. It was like I was deflating with tears. It was not fair Brant had so many things to do and I always known he was destined for greatness. This could not be it we were just getting to the good part. We had finally become a family and now it was over.

Then it came like a wave over me what a beautiful place. I could imagine Brant and his friends here playing volleyball on the beach and swimming in the small pools and sunbathing on the sandbars. This would be how he would want to go having fun with his friends.

My son had been in the water three days almost to the exact hour before he rose from the darkness to be found. Was God telling me something? Just like his son died and rose in three days later. Was God telling me that he would take care of Brant for me now? I took this as a sign from God that this was so. I found some comfort in that. That God would take care of Brant now. No more trouble sleeping nor remembering. No more nightmares for Brant, Martha could not hurt him anymore. He was with God now and he would be all right. It was little solace then but at least it was something. I cried for a long time on that log until it finally dawned on me that the rest of my children needed me and I needed to get back to them. So we left the beautiful beach behind and the siren from the ambulance disappeared as we drove away.

Chapter 25

GOING HOME

The college had called and opened Brant's dorm room for us because we had decided to get his stuff on the way home. It was better to do it now than to have to come back. I had lots of help with my mom and dad, my brothers and their wives, we were all there. I felt like I had been kicked in the gut by a mule but we needed to get this over with and it would not take as long with this many people.

I had not seen Brant's new dorm room and he had three roommates. One of them was there and directed us to Brant's room. There were four bedrooms in this small apartment one for each of them. This is not how I wanted to see his new apartment. I felt like I had cried the tears out but only a couple minutes in his room I could smell Brant's cologne and that was it.

I ran down to the parking lot. I felt like I was choking. I am not one for public crying so I walked to the far end of the parking lot and back. I could not take it. It took only about a half hour to clean out his room and gather all his stuff. When we finally left it was like my body had gone limp. I had no strength left in me. I needed to get home to tell the kids before they found out some other way. Stupid phones it seemed everything was on Facebook before you could actually tell people something. I needed to tell them face-to-face. This was something I needed to be there for in person.

As I got nearer to home I could feel a sense of dread about telling them their brother was dead. I was sure they knew that by now in their heads but to hear it made it real. We had enough bad news and now they would get the worse. Worse yet I had failed them. I could not bring Brant home like I had always done. There was nothing I could have done but it felt like I had failed them anyway. A dad was supposed to make everything right, he was supposed to protect his children. I would have gladly traded my life for any of my children's but I had not even been given the chance. I had not been there to save him. I felt cheated. I was not even given the choice of my life for Brant's. It was not fair.

As I drove into the yard, my feet felt like chunks of concrete as I opened the door. The kids jumped up to meet me at the door. I looked into their eyes and I could see it. They knew what was coming. I felt ashamed. I failed them and they would feel pain again. I told them then and we all sat down watching a movie but not really seeing it at all. It would be a quiet evening because the wait was over and we had lost one of our own. We knew life would never be the same again as we all sat remembering the good times in our heads and saying nothing. We understood the hard part was to come. None of us wanted to see anyone. We just wanted to be left alone to grieve. But we all knew this would not happen. Our private lives would end now with the funeral and our funny guy was not around to make us laugh anymore.

I was not prepared at all for a funeral but who is. This had come out of the blue and landed on me. I had never had to plan a funeral before and did not realize how much there was to plan. It was something we had never talked about, why would we he was only nineteen. I was not in any condition to handle all the questions like what kind of songs did he like and what scripture passages were his favorites.

Since we were Catholics, there would be a mass and there was a lot to do before the funeral. There was also food and how much to order and what you wanted to serve, it was too much for me. I should be spending time with my kids and instead I was dealing with this. My family helped me through it. I felt more like an empty shell. I felt hollow inside. I felt such sadness, a deep all-encompassing dark sadness that seemed to fill me up and choke me.

I had to pick out a casket and above all I had to do it fast because now Brant's name would be released to the papers. The sheriff had told me there was nothing he could do about that. Why not? Why could a parent not keep his son's name from hitting the papers? They had no idea the damage that would do. I knew Martha would come and even though there was a restraining order she would get around it. She always did.

Why did I have to even think about anything but getting through this, yet here I was still planning for Martha to show up and cause drama. Which at this point I could not handle. I had enough. I could not handle any more. I had come to the end of my patience, my control over myself was over. Why should I have to plan around Martha, would that never end?

Brant would not want her there of that I was sure and what about the other children why should they have to deal with the death of their brother and the possibility of seeing her. Which I was sure would be a trigger for all of them seeing her in their safe place. She was not allowed here. There was a restraining order against her until they all turned eighteen. She would come I knew it in my mind even though my lawyers told me it was not possible. Yes, I did have to talk to my lawyers too. To ease my mind, they were going to provide an officer to escort her out if she showed up. I felt better about that. I could not handle that, her, now. I was just trying to figure out how the children and I were going to get through the funeral.

The people at the funeral home were amazing they walked us through it and they really cared which is something you do not see much anymore. My family was awesome too, my brothers and my parents took care of almost everything except the specific things I had to do. I had to schedule the funeral as early as possible to give Martha the least chance of making it. The other reason was that since Brant had been in the water that long the funeral needed to be as soon as possible. I would never get to see Brant again because after the autopsy he would be sealed in a black plastic bag and placed in the casket. His casket would have to have an extra liner in it because his body could not be properly prepared for burial.

The children and I would not get to see him. We would not get to say goodbye. We would not get to hold his hand and say goodbye. It did not seem like much but it would have meant a lot to us. The couple days flew by and I felt even worse that I had not given people time to get there for the funeral. It had only been a couple of days and most people from far away would not even know about it. It would be on a Friday. Brant's high school let out classes so the children could attend his funeral. Even now almost two years after his graduation he was greatly missed.

The day came and none of us were ready for it. It was a drab cloudy day and we had decided to hold a small family service at his grave site before mass began in case Martha showed up. At this time everyone had assured me she would not. After all his name had only been released a day ago to the papers. Brant would be buried in the little town of less than a hundred people. It really was just a church and a couple of bars. It was a large beautiful church with a high steeple and it held a lot of people. It had a marvelous alter with beautiful life-size statues in the front on a beautifully carved showcase. Many people came for miles just to have their wedding there. It also seemed somewhat poetic that this was the very town he had explored with his Grandma when he was little. He belonged here.

As I drove up to the fence of the little graveyard in the country on the little hill, there they were, Martha and ten of her family members, just as calm as you could be. I backed up and drove to the far side of the cemetery and parked. I could not believe it after all my planning they were here. I could not deal with this it was way too much. The one person that did not belong here and there she was. She always hated him and tried to kill him herself several times. She had put him in a mental hospital and did her best to destroy his life and she was here. I could not handle this and what about the kids, they did not need this, today of all days. We spent the last days talking about how much they did not want her here. She did not deserve to be here. Brant did not want her here.

My family and the priest were here now. I would talk to the priest and we would do this later. I could not handle it and the anger within me was mounting. The priest had walked up behind my vehicle and I told the kids to stay inside. They did not have to deal with this I would take care of it. We would go to the church and have the service later when they were gone. I did not need a confrontation today.

As I came around the back of my pickup to talk to the priest, I saw it. I did not know how to describe the scene in front of me, Martha's family had descended upon mine waving a paper in the air and yelling that they had a legal right to be here. Now as far as I knew, no one had even talked to them and here they were making a huge scene at the gravesite of my son who just died such a horrible death.

I broke. I suffered too much too long and this day, I could take it no more. I would bury them all right here. We were in a cemetery after all. The world turned red and I could not breathe. I yelled out in a voice that was not my own, "Get the hell out of here! Brant would not want you here!" My brother Anton would tell me later that when I yelled it felt as if the very earth of the cemetery trembled.

I saw my brothers ready to jump in for they were just as appalled as I was. I did not need help I would finish it here and now and it would be over. As I yelled the only thing between me and Martha's family was the priest. He was a small man and could not have weighed a hundred pounds. He stood his ground even though his eyes showed the fear of being mauled by a stampeding elephant. I could not tell if he was so scared he could not move or stood his ground to stop me. You could see it in his eyes that he thought his life was over.

I could feel Brant with me whispering in my ear, you got this dad. Then someone grabbed my arm and broke my stride, it was my lawyer who had become my friend since the whole thing started. I was shaking and he was trying to pull me back behind my pickup and he kept saying, "Brant would not want this!" This was not helping at all because Brant had been whispering in my ear the opposite but then he said, "Think of the other children, what would they do if you were in jail." Finally it clicked and I followed him behind the pickup.

The testosterone hit me then and I could not breathe and I felt as if I would fall. I put my hand on the pickup to steady myself. Then my lawyer filled me in that Martha had slid a court hearing in at the end of the day with a new judge that did not know the situation. The judge had told my lawyer that she was sorry but she had just signed it because it was the end of the day and had not read up on the case.

A "sorry. "That is what I get! A sorry for making this horrible day even worse. I wanted to hit someone, anyone, but mostly them on the other side of the pickup. My lawyer had slowed me down and sanity started settling in. Once my breathing had slowed, I felt sick. We would have our service now, now that they had gone, and then go to the church.

My lawyer asked if there was anything left he could do and I said, "Keep them out of my sight because if I see them again I will not be responsible for what I will do to them." My lawyer nodded in agreement and assigned several officers to escort Martha and her family into the church because of course they were trying to make a scene.

While my lawyer was talking to me, Martha and her family had their own service at the gravesite and then they left to attend the funeral. They had not left one flower or card or anything whatsoever for Brant when they left which showed that they had not come for him, only for themselves. This was all about them and causing more grief for the children by getting to them any way they could.

Little did I know but as my lawyer was talking to me, Martha and her sisters and mother drove by and flicked off my children sitting in the pickup, from their car. It was not directed at me but at the children. They had actually told my children to fuck off at their brother's funeral. Can you believe it? The children were the ones who told me about it later that Martha and her sisters were laughing as they drove by and did it. It made me so sick to think about it later when they told me the story. What kind of animals do something like that? The pure black evilness of their actions haunt me to this day. I was ashamed. I could not even protect my son in the grave from Martha. I felt not only the pain of his loss, but defeat again as well. Had I seen it happen with my own eyes, no force on heaven or earth could have stopped me from wiping them from the face of this planet!

The church was packed when we arrived and people were standing in the back because there was not a seat to be found. I was utterly exhausted when we arrived at the church. The morning had completely drained me. I had never been totally out of control like that before but this was the worse day I had ever faced in my life. We were seated in the front pew with all of our family behind us.

We were not front pew Catholics. You would always find us in the last row way in the back. We always sat in the balcony in the back because Dad had always said we were closer to God that way. So this made us even more uncomfortable as the mass began. Thoughts were running through my mind: Would Martha and her family make a scene, would they try to hug the children at communion time. Here in the front we were vulnerable. Brant would not want them here. He would not like it at all.

I had written a eulogy for Brant. I spent every waking minute since his death thinking about it. It needed to be short but there was so much to say. I finally finished it that morning and there had only been one person I knew of to read it; my cousin Lucy. She was always good under pressure and had a mother's voice and she would do it. Her sister Kate would do the readings. It was a horrible thing to do to someone to have them read such heartfelt words at a time like this and not break down but that is what family is all about. If you are asked, you cannot back down. I had finally finished it that morning I had spent all night on it which was just as well who could sleep anyway.

The eulogy went by fast and my cousin did a superb job reading it.

"What can I say about Brant? If you met him you liked him. He had a way about him that brought sunshine everywhere he went. I would say that it was a God-given light that surrounded him and he used it to inspire so many others. He loved spending time with his family, his brother and sisters, and especially his grandpa who was his hero. Likewise my son was a hero to me. As a parent I always wanted my children to turn out better than me. Brant was. He was not only my oldest son but my hero and my very, very best friend.

I can still see him now in this very town walking down the street as a little boy with his tuft of white hair blowing in the wind beside his wonderful Grandma exploring the town. Even then I had seen how special he was. He always waited for Grandma. He never left her behind.

Sports and school were a big part of his life. He was always on the honor roll and loved participating in the science fair. He was also in many plays and loved to make people laugh. He had been on a championship baseball team and a championship football team. Being on a team meant the world to him. He was also a long-distance runner in cross country and ran track. He had qualified for the state many times. There was never a time in his life when he did not give it 110 percent. He never ever wanted to let anyone down.

There was never a time when he would not stop in his busy life to share a word or two with a friend or even a stranger passing by. I still remember his many track meets and seeing him stop on his way to a race to talk to one of the younger children. They liked to follow him around and ask him questions about how he was so fast. It made him late to the race many times but it did not bother him. He had his priorities straight and there was no race worth running if he could not brighten someone's day with a kind word.

His friends meant the world to him and there was nothing he would not do for them. He had many friends, as you can see by the huge crowd gathered here today, and believe me when I say that every one of you was his friend. That was the way he was. If you talked to him for five minutes or five hours, even once in his life, you were his friend. Many times in my life I waited for him just because he was holding the door for a woman holding a child or an old lady that could not quite get it done by herself. It was his selflessness that made him special.

I watched him inspire so many people to do such amazing things. Even here now I know his light will live on in each one of you and in all the people his life had touched. Because he made a difference in every life he touched. I am very proud to be his father and I would like to thank each and everyone one of you for being here today to honor my son on his last day and so I say goodbye to my son, my hero, my friend. I love you very much.

Then it was open for anyone who wanted to say anything about Brant and several of his friends got up and shared nice memories of him. During all of this I was on pins and needles wondering if and when Martha's family would cause a scene but they never did.

I found out later that they had tried to start trouble but the law officers that were escorting them kept them from doing anything.

They would also try to come over to the church center afterwards where we had a meal for everyone. Luckily the court order only said that they could attend the funeral and the sheriff had to escort them out of the county because they were causing so much trouble. They did not trust them to leave on their own.

It was the end of the church service and everyone was singing the last song and it had truly been, aside from the disaster at the cemetery, a beautiful service. There was no casket so in its place we had a blown up picture of Brant in front of the altar. One of our favorites from his senior pictures. I missed that hug from the last time I had seen him alive and though I was one to stand back and not make a scene I could not help it. As I stood up to leave with the music playing I walked to the front of the altar picked up his picture and gave it a hug. It would be the last time and this would be as close as I would get to one last hug to say goodbye. My brother Anton would tell me later that he had held it together until then and asked me why I had done it. I told him it was just something I had to do.

Afterwards at the center I finally sat down and relaxed because it was over. The thought of Martha and her family ruining Brant's final day had loomed over me since his death like a dark cloud. They had shown up anyway and made their scene but it was over now. As I sat there, my legs felt like jelly and I was unable to stand as a line began to form to come shake my hand and tell me how much they had liked Brant and was so sorry he was gone. It lasted over an hour and I wondered when the line would stop. So many people had come to see him one last time. Brant had his last big party. He would have thought it was grand.

I would find some strength later and was drawn into many conversations with his friends about adventures they had and how exciting it was to have him around. They told me he was the kindest soul that they knew and he would always listen to a friend in trouble and make you laugh somehow. Towards the end of a long afternoon a couple of his best friends from high school came over and invited me to the high school football field where they would plant a tree for Brant. This was the first time I had heard about it and said that I would gladly come.

So we loaded up the kids, myself, and my mother and headed to the football field. As we drew near I could not believe my eyes it looked like there was a football game or something going on. The entire town had turned out to plant this tree for Brant. The sun had come out and it was setting on a beautiful fall day. The football field was deep green and around the outside of the field was a row of trees. At the end of this was where they planted Brant's tree.

I had never seen anything like it before or since. There were the little kids Brant always talked to at the track meets and all his friends and their parents and his teachers and a lot of people I did not even know. There were hundreds of them and they had all come because Brant had somehow touched their lives. He had only gone to school there two years but you would have believed he had spent his entire life there.

I was speechless. I was hugged over and over and shook hands until I thought might possibly faint. Then one of his friends got up to speak as the others dug the hole. Brant had only twenty kids in his grade and just about all of them were there to say goodbye to him. As she began to speak my throat tightened and felt like I might pass out. His classmates were passing out small bits of paper and told everyone to write their greatest memory of Brant on it and place it in the hole. They had to dig the hole deeper and deeper because all the paper would not fit in it because so many people had come. To watch the young and the old and short and tall walk up from all directions to put their piece of paper in this hole made my heart melt. I thought there could be no greater tribute to a person's life than this. To have an entire town put up a monument for him was more than any parent could ask for.

Finally, it was near dark before they got the tree in the ground and to think this tree was planted on a mound of love that Brant had bestowed in the short time he was here. It was a beautiful little tree and chokingly I thanked everyone for coming and said that he had considered every person here, his friend. This was surreal. These people did not even know what Brant had gone through, they only knew him as he was and yet he had moved them so much that they all came here for him.

As I sat there and the people slowly disappeared after telling lots of stories about Brant. I looked at the little tree among the giant trees that surrounded it. It was the smallest but the most beautiful of all of them. I thought, how like Brant was the little tree, so small and yet it seemed to dwarf the trees around it somehow with its beauty. The little tree is bigger now and in the fall it is still the most beautiful tree there but what do you expect with so much love beneath it.

A few days later I would get another call from his college friends and they too were going to have a memorial for Brant, since most of them had not been able to come to the funeral, at the college. So again we made the trek to the college. The whole time reminding myself that I had never gone there before without seeing Brant. We were met by the Dean of the college and his staff. They had all come to the memorial. I had never seen that before but they were there as Brant was a part of the honor society. I was very surprised when I entered the room.

It was a large room and it was full so they had to bring more chairs for us. I saw teachers, students, and there were even people he had worked with at the grocery store. It was just as astonishing as the other memorials that Brant had touched so many lives in such a short time. Many of them got up and told stories of crazy things that they had done at college. Even the people he worked with got up and told stories of how great he was to work with and how fast time flew with Brant making jokes the whole time. Even his teachers got up and told everyone what a joy it had been just to read his papers and that he had been turning in fourth-year level papers even though he was only a sophomore. Afterwards they had a mass at a small church on campus followed by lighting Chinese lanterns on the beach where it had all happened.

When we arrived on the beach it did not seem as bad as before. The beach was full of his friends some in groups crying and others laughing sharing memories of Brant. It was a beautiful warm night with only a slight breeze which kept the mosquitoes away. As it grew dark and they started to light the lanterns, it became quite comical. Many lanterns started to catch on fire and others just hit the ground but just when we thought none of them would get off the ground at the very end the last lantern took off. It went up and up and it was beautiful as everyone watched it fly down the river. I thought Brant would have loved this. His friends here having a good time all because of him. I had the feeling that lantern was just like Brant, he too was that one in a hundred that flew above the rest and made you feel good about yourself. That one bright light in the darkness.

I always knew my son was destined for great things. I felt cheated since his death, thinking that I would never get to see him do these great things that I knew he was capable of. He could have done anything. Brant had only been limited by his own imagination. I had seen him time and again overcome unbelievable obstacles and still achieve his goals. But here, now after all I had seen, the lives he had touched, even in his death, I realized all he had done.

In such a short time he had touched so many people and made their lives better with a smile or a joke all the while fighting his own demons. I was so proud of him. He had accomplished something marvelous indeed. He had friends, hundreds of them, and he would live on in each of them. The stories and the memories he left would

Chapter 26

DAD

The days after the funeral were spent opening letters. All the mail that was sent consoling us on our loss. They were hard to read but we read each and every one. There were heartfelt letters from friends and people who had not made it to the funeral or the memorials. I even heard from old bosses and other people I had known in my life. I got mail from people I did not even know. People who had met Brant at a track or cross country meet. I read mail from people who had lost their own children at a young age and from relatives that I did not even know I had. It was a humbling feeling to see how many people liked Brant and remembered him. But after all, he really was hard to forget. Most of these people had only known him for an hour and yet they had seen how special he was.

I would spend a long time trying to find the words to put on his tombstone. I felt they should be something special not just the norm. We had a priest once when I was an altar boy who referred to our little town as Camelot since it seemed to be green most of the time. Since Brant loved history, I decided to write something that a knight might have on his headstone. This is what I came up with:

Here lies Brant the adventurer, poet, and friend. I am proud of the boy who became the man I always wanted to be. We will miss our shining star that burned too bright and too fast. May his immortal light shine on us on our darkest nights. We will always miss you my son, my hero, my friend. Love, Dad

I wanted it to say just how I felt about him. I wanted him to know how proud I was of him. It felt like Brant needed something special on his stone; something private from me. This would be his final medal. I hope that it did him justice because I loved him so very much.

In the days that followed, I admit I was depressed. I felt like doing nothing. Just let the world go by without me. I did not feel like eating or doing anything that took effort. I wanted to live in the dark and sleep. I knew, as did the children, that we would never be right again. It was like a wagon wheel with a missing spoke it would not run right. My father saw this and would show up at the house quite often and barge in and open the curtains and drag me outside to do something.

He already lived through this once. His one and only sister had died at a young age from a high fever that doctors never figured out why. He would return again and again and we would talk. I grew closer to my father than I had ever been. I had put him on a pedestal my whole life. He was like John Wayne. Someone who was to be respected and not really known. He had been good to me. We were a father and son in the old ways where children always talked to their parent with respect but never talked about real things like life and feelings. Now since Brant died, we shared a common bond in his death that was more than just a father and son relationship. We were somewhat kindred spirits. Although my father had lost his sister so long ago, I found that he had needed to talk to someone about it after all these years. Now we shared this loss with each other because we both understood how the other felt. We were more like long lost friends now than father and son.

Then one day about four months after Brant's funeral the second wave of grief had hit me hard and dad had dragged me out of the house. We had been talking for a while about the crops and weather and such. Then he got in his truck and was about to leave. I put my hand on the open window and a feeling came over me. Now our family was not one to talk about our feelings much and I never talked to dad about them before, but there was something I needed to ask and so I did, "Dad does this ever get better."

After all, he had been through this before and I wanted to know now, because I was at the end of my rope. He turned and looked at me and I saw the pain in his eyes, the same pain I was feeling. In that moment I saw the great rock, that was my father, break, and he became human to me. Just a man, just like me.

He said as he looked away down a road that was not there, "There are days when I still tell my little sister hi as I walk by her room and I can see her sitting there. I give her a wave and she waves back. So no, the pain does not get better. It is something that you just learn to live with." I saw a tear roll down his cheek and then he sped away. A week later he would die from something the doctors could not figure out but I knew. It was a broken heart, a heart that could not take the death of two so young in one lifetime. So now we would have to live without our inspiration and our rock.

My brother Anton wanted me to write a eulogy for our father to be read at the funeral. I was not sure about it. I had written one for Brant and people had liked it so I said I would. I spent two days on it but the words would not come. Finally it was the night before the funeral and still I could not put into words how I felt about my dad.

I fell asleep on the tear stained paper still pen in hand. I dreamed of my father at a younger age. How he looked when I was a kid. He was riding his old brown horse, his favorite. He was just how I remembered him in his straw hat and sleeveless shirt. He always carried a bull whip for stubborn cattle and a rifle for sneaky coyotes. He was riding away from me into the sunset calling out looking for something.

Then I heard him calling Brant's name as he weaved up and down the hills. Now I understood why he had left us. He was making sure Brant had gotten where he was supposed to go. Watching my back just like he had always done. Then I awoke with light shining on my face and quickly jotted down what I had dreamed. I also added a few things that can only be said between a son and his father.

I think maybe God had given me a little window into heaven that night. Maybe he felt sorry for me or just wanted to put me at ease. That dream gives me solace still and it is still so vivid in my memory like I was really there. It gives me great comfort that they are together now and I am grateful for that dream.

In the days, months, and years to come I would find out my father was right. Time does not heal all wounds and pain does not end. You learn to live with it and it becomes a part of you. With each bad thing that happens to you, you change. There is no way to go back and be the person you were before it happened. You will however come to cherish that pain because it reminds you of the ones you have lost. There are more good memories than bad.

There were times when I thought I was all cried out and that the pain in the pit of my stomach was too deep to cry anymore. But the tears would come again and that would be good. It is cathartic. In the long run, it is better to let it out than hold it in. I still see Brant now and again when something funny happens or in a memory that pops into my head. I see him in his little nephews when they fall asleep when I am babysitting them. I see him in his brother and sisters and his friends. People may say that is strange but I think that is all part of living with it and I will never forget him. I still go to the little cemetery on his birthday or holidays and leave a carved pumpkin or a Christmas tree for him and dad. It is just something I do to let them know I did not forget about them.

Chapter 27
THE CANDLES

I still light the candles for Brant every Sunday after church just like he always did. It is the one thing that is still constant in my life. I light three candles for him. Every Sunday I carefully take the light from the dying candle and transport it to a new candle so the flame never dies. Many people have asked me why I light three candles but I have never told anyone why.

I have decided to share this secret with you because I feel that you should know. You see the secret of the candles is why I have shared my son's story with you. That you will understand just what these candles meant to him and mean to me.

The first candle I light is for those who have gone before us like Brant and Dad, Grandma and Grandpa, and everyone else who have died before us. I pray that their souls get to heaven and that they are happy now. Between you and me, if they do not make it, I feel none of us will.

The second candle I light is for us, the survivors, as I call them. Those of us still on earth like my children and my mom and the rest of the family and me. I especially pray for anyone who is sick and in need of special prayers. I also pray for help for us to make it through another day and deal with all the grief we have suffered.

The third and final candle is an extra special candle that I refer to as Brant's light. Brant had that special something, that certain something that was more like a feeling when you where around him. I would call it a God-given power, the power to inspire hope and inspiration through laughter. The way he showed a never ending, unconditional love for another human being. He instilled such inspiration in you to do things that you never even knew you could. He did it in such a way as you would not even know it happened. He believed in you so much that you became more than you even knew you could be just so you would not disappoint him.

I believe that is why God needed him because his gift became so great that a human body could not hold it anymore. I believe that God gave him wings so he could reach more people than he could here on earth. Brant's power to inspire was a gift from God. Like all God's gifts they come to us like a shooting star. They burn fast and bright and light up the heavens and then they are gone. Leaving behind them wonder and awe. No matter how much we would like to keep them they are only here to light the way. The rest is up to us.

This is why I light his candle, this candle is for you. For all the children and parents or anyone who fights the darkness everyday looking for the light. This candle is for the children locked up in psychiatric hospitals everywhere who feel safer locked in there than at home. This candle is for all the moms and dads who fight for themselves and their children to keep them safe from the monsters of this world. It is for the little guy that is told he cannot do it. But most of all, I light this candle for each and every one of you so that you know you are not alone.

I know what it's like to fight the darkness and feel all alone. So I light this candle so that Brant may find you and share with you that strength, that God-given power of his to find the light and beat the darkness. So do me a favor, when the night becomes too dark or you feel so alone that you cannot see the light, light a candle and say a prayer. I do not care if you have never prayed before it is quite easy. Just ask for help.

Your candle does not need to be in a church nor a synagogue nor inside any religious structure. It does not matter if it the candle is big or small because that has nothing to do with its purpose. Its purpose is so my son can find you and give you that power and strength to become more than you ever thought you could be. To fight the darkness and win. It is possible, believe me I have been through it.

So do yourself a favor, light a candle, it really does not matter if you believe, but try it anyway. What have you got to lose? We could all use a little help sometimes. Because I believe that if enough of us light candles the darkness will have nowhere to hide. Then maybe, just maybe, we will all become more than we ever thought we could be. Then what a world that would be, a world bathed in that heavenly light, Brant's light.